D0100577

The

DIGNITY DOCTRINE

The

DIGNITY DOCTRINE

Rational Relations in an Irrational World

MARK C. COLEMAN

SelectBooks, Inc.
New York

Copyright © 2020 by Mark C. Coleman

All rights reserved. Published in the United States of America. No part of this book may be reproduced or transmitted in any form or by any means, graphic, electronic, or mechanical, including photocopying, recording, taping, or by any information storage or retrieval system, without the permission in writing from the publisher.

This edition published by SelectBooks, Inc.

For information address SelectBooks, Inc., New York, New York.

First Edition

ISBN 978-1-59079-505-7

Library of Congress Cataloging-in-Publication Data

Names: Coleman, Mark C., author.
Title: The dignity doctrine : rational relations in an irrational world / Mark C. Coleman.
Description: First edition. | New York : SelectBooks, [2020] | Includes bibliographical references and index. | Summary: "Author explores how business and consumers address the effects of human-induced ecological degradation, climate change, and negative influences of advanced technologies on our individual freedoms, dignity, and security. He advises that improving our self-respect and our respect for others, including Earth and its limited precious resources, will inspire our ingenuity to create a more sustainable world"--Provided by publisher.
Identifiers: LCCN 2019055906 (print) | LCCN 2019055907 (ebook) | ISBN 9781590795057 (paperback) | ISBN 9781590795019 (ebook)
Subjects: LCSH: Environmental responsibility. | Sustainability. | Sustainable development. | Social interaction. | Respect.
Classification: LCC GE195.7 .C638 2020 (print) | LCC GE195.7 (ebook) | DDC 363.7--dc23
LC record available at https://lccn.loc.gov/2019055906
LC ebook record available at https://lccn.loc.gov/2019055907

Cover and book design by Janice Benight

Manufactured in the United States of America
10 9 8 7 6 5 4 3 2 1

Contents

Preface and Acknowledgments

I'd like to first thank you, the reader, for taking the personal time and investment to choose this title amid so many great books out there. I hope this book provides you with some valuable insight and perspective on how we each have a distinct role to serve and how people can constructively work together toward creating a more peaceful, just, and sustainable world.

Writing and publishing is a team sport. I'm honored to have worked closely with an incredible group of professionals, colleagues, friends, and family whose influence and support made this book possible.

Through my own writing experience and what I've learned from other authors over the past few years, I've grown to understand and appreciate the level of motivation and desire that must exist deep within one's soul to take on the challenge of expressing oneself through writing. Published authors know, however, that motivation and desire alone are not enough. We need a team of contrarians, optimists, truthtellers, and perfectionists who challenge us to be at our best—and to always improve. During the process, we must also look within ourselves to kindle virtues of patience, humility, excellence, grace, authenticity, and courage since our motivation needs to be consistently manifested and directed by the right mindset to shape a worthy manuscript. I'm grateful for the right confluence of personal will and skill and a highly supportive team that has given me this opportunity to publish my third book.

I must begin by giving my utmost gratitude, love, and admiration to the key captain of my team, my wife Aileen

McNabb-Coleman, who reminds me through her actions every day that happiness is a clear conscious choice. Through Aileen's relentless will to thrive, she has overcome more challenges in the past ten years than many people see in a lifetime. Aileen's journey, captured in this book, is an emotional and inspirational story of personal strength, resiliency, growth, and rejoice in life. Aileen, my life is enriched and enlivened with you in it. I love you. I'm continuously amazed by your spirit. Thank you for all that you are and do for us and our family.

I'm overwhelmed by how great life can be, particularly when we choose to see and celebrate in all its glory. I'm so honored and so grateful to be the father of Owen and Neal, my two boys who are literally growing up before my eyes. Our children are our future, and I'm so excited to be witnessing the growth of my sons, cautiously discovering who they are, yet clearly defined individually and anchored by their own sense of integrity, independence and intellect. I love you, boys, and feel forever blessed to have you and your mom at my side. You are my inspiration and will always have my deepest admiration.

This book is a personal accomplishment on many levels, but it is also the result of months of preparation and hard work of writing, editing, with all forms of publishing support from the incredible team at SelectBooks. In 2012 SelectBooks published my first book, *The Sustainability Generation: The Politics of Change and Why Personal Accountability is Essential NOW!* When I learned that I could work again with the amazing team at SelectBooks I jumped at the chance to do so. Simply put, they push me to be a better, more thoughtful, and deliberate writer. Thank you Kenzi, Nancy, and Kenichi. The focus, guidance, creativity, and expertise you provided shaped my manuscript into the high-quality and meaningful book this has become. Thank you for believing in me and my work. I'm ecstatic that we worked together again. Your support and friendship mean a great deal to me. I'm grateful and look forward to our continued collaborations.

To this end, I must also give admiration and thanks to Bill Gladstone and his team at Waterside Productions, Inc. Bill had introduced me to SelectBooks before 2012. More than a year ago, I reached out to Bill and let him know that I was well into developing a manuscript for a third book. With my excitement evident, Bill pushed me, as he does in his pragmatic way, to hone my idea into a clear value position. Bill is an agent who not only knows the industry extremely well, but who spends time getting to know authors and publishers as people, not just as a business. Bill and his team supported this project from the onset. I'm grateful for having Bill and the Waterside Productions team engaged and supportive of me as well as this book.

Special thanks to Jon Reis, Deidre Mollura, and Jacob Mroczek of Jon Reis Photography for their professionalism and skill in capturing my portrait photo for the book. I'm not someone who generally likes photos of himself, but Jon, Deidre, and Jacob did a terrific job.

I'd like to acknowledge the contribution and support of numerous colleagues, friends, and family who provided me with independent, objective, and thoughtful feedback during all phases of the writing and publishing process. A very special thanks to Fernando Paiz, Monica Olveira, Laura Ponticello, Rajiv Ramchandra, Denny Minano, Joe Zagrobelny, David Tarino, Maria Fronseca, Dinis Guarda, Eric McLamb and Stelios Vogiatzis. I'm indebted to have you as great colleagues, mentors, teachers, and friends in my life. Thank you for everything you've done in support of this project. I could not have reached this milestone without your honest and critical reviews and insightful contributions.

I've come to realize that writing for me is selfish and therapeutic. As I worked on my manuscript, it dawned on me that writing, at least in my case, is a process of continual self-evaluation and personal growth. Through writing I'm able to exercise thought and emotion and deconstruct elements of my past and present while being mindful of how I want to shape the future. This is not something I need to delve into any deeper, other than to say I've realized that in my writing I'm unconsciously working to understand myself and the world and making an effort to continually evolve and grow as a human being.

As I have worked to improve this craft, I now see the arts and other forms of self-expression in a different light. In the act of making art, we discover who we are. The creative translation and transformation of oneself is never complete. The canvas we create is only one reflection of our being. What emerges as a stanza of music, a self-portrait in watercolors, or a carefully constructed narrative from our soul, never captures the depth of our full being or the entire character of who we are. Yet writers, musicians, artists, photographers, performers, and many in other fields of work continue to express themselves in hopes that we will get closer to our understanding of ourselves and others. For those who choose to create with their hands, minds, and heart—thank you for sharing yourself so truly and openly with the world. In the act of self-expression, may we all find that we have more in common than not, as well as a creative way to bring joy and hope to ourselves and those around us. The world is richer and more diverse with us in it!

Introduction

A human being is a part of the whole, called by us "Universe," a part limited in time and space. He experiences himself, his thoughts and feelings as something separate from the rest—a kind of optical delusion of his consciousness. The striving to free oneself from this delusion is the one issue of true religion. Not to nourish it but to try to overcome it is the way to reach the attainable measure of peace of mind.

—ALBERT EINSTEIN
February 12, 1950
Letter to Mr. Robert S. Marcus of the World Jewish Congress

I recently turned 43 years old. During four decades of life, I have had times of success and times of struggling. Like billions of other people, I have witnessed society at some of its finest and most wicked moments. In the act of writing this book I came across the quote by Albert Einstein. This quote has stuck with me because it speaks so eloquently about the human condition. We are all alive for just a small slice of time. Many things shape the perception we have of the world during our lifetime. Our politics, family, religion, community, and education each influence our worldview and, to a certain extent, our behaviors.

With such dynamic and vast stimulation, it is easy for any of us to be lured and consumed by an "optical delusion" of reality, as if our being is separate from those around us. Ultimately, however, our self-worth, ethos, identity, and impact are manifested through our own design and doing. As Einstein points out, the act of freeing oneself from the delusion that we are separate from the Universe is how we can attain true peace of mind. I believe the true meaning of dignity is revealed when we selflessly open ourselves up

1

to others and accept that none of us are alone in the world but are all intimately and intrinsically interconnected in time and space.

Unfortunately, there are people walking this earth who are unhappy and feel hopeless and estranged from friends, family, and society. These people need our help. Some are truly lost, reclusive and hidden from daily life. We do not often see them, and do not spend much time or energy thinking of them, let alone seeking them out. Some others are in our face, seemingly motivated to bring us down to their level of misery and waywardness. These folks are often charismatic, smart, and well liked. They are also dangerous narcissists who care only for themselves.

We live at a time when many people are fearful and starving for authentic leadership. This fact is what makes the current state of divisive politics in the United States and throughout the world so disconcerting. When fear is front and center in people's lives, individual and collective freedoms are at risk.

Dictators rule by maintaining an environment whereby the masses are anxious and uncertain of their future. Tyrants drive the political discourse to the point of dysfunction and collapse. They covertly and deviously work to shape the dialogue and narrative of daily life, emboldening their stature, self-absorption, and evil intentions.

Fear ignites and fuels dictators, terrorists, and other bad actors. History has a running log of affluent societies that have fallen and imploded because fear got the best of society. When people lose sight of what is honest and true they seek out some form of comfort and certainty. If a sense of security is not attained, fear can breed cynicism, distrust, passivity, and ultimately panic among the masses.

Why is the pursuit and attainment of peace more challenging than conflict and war? Humans are fundamentally flawed. We are continually at war with each other and ourselves; we never seem content to be fully at peace. The world is comprised of more than 7.7 billion people representative of different religions, ideology, race, sexual identity, color, and creed. At face value, humans seem to appreciate the idea that the earth is streaming richly with a diversity of life. Why, then, can we not simply accept the fact that every person on Earth is as unique as a snowflake and that our differences are what actually make the world interesting and brimming with energy and life?

It does not take that much to rock the stability meter of a society. Today, this meter bounces back and forth at pace with a president's tweets. The sitting president chooses, quite deliberately, to address meaty issues like immigration, money laundering, Russian hacking of elections, and nuclear war with Korea, among many others, in the often cryptic but always boisterous text of 280 characters or less. The daily (if not hourly or minute-by-minute) tweet tirade by the president is covered by national media outlets as "Breaking News," providing justification and stature to his chosen method of social influence. To be clear, dictators like a microphone. Twitter is this president's microphone. Social media has essentially weaponized the presidency. Moreover, as if Twitter and other social media channels were not loud enough, the news media magnifies the weaponized messages of the sitting president and his colleagues to all the corners of the Earth.

Given the microphone, these leaders will continue to wield it at any chance they get to draw attention to themselves and their agenda. The chaos and confusion that is created is part of a deliberate strategy they have to knock a swift blow to society, leaving it shaken, unsteady, and ready to be pounced upon and shaped in an image of their (not our) liking. Fear is extremely powerful. Don't be naïve or foolish enough to believe that there are not people in this world, some very close to home, who want you to be on edge, fearful of your future, fearing for your life.

In his 1933 presidential inauguration address, Franklin D. Roosevelt spoke the famous words, "The only thing we have to fear is fear itself." I have written this book, my third, as a personal credo, as well as one which I believe can shape the betterment of humanity. In times of great prosperity as well as despair, we need to remember who we the people are. As FDR said:

> [T]his Nation is not merely a Nation of independence, but it is, if we are to survive, bound to be a Nation of interdependence—town and City, and North and South, East and West. That is our goal, and that goal will be understood by the people of this country no matter where we live.
>
> FDR's acceptance speech to the Democratic Convention
> July 2, 1932, during the Great Depression[1]

In our time of anxiety about the earth's biosphere, we have extended our interdependence to global nations and include our entire humanity and our living planet itself.

In good times and bad, we are all the force by which humanity can lift itself higher, out of any hole or above any ridgeline, as we see farther into the possibilities of the future than ever before.

It is in the humility and power of humanity that we find greatness, individually and collectively as a society. *The Dignity Doctrine* presents principles and methods for creating partnerships of purpose, impact, and distinction. Such partnerships can be a marriage, a friendship, a business alliance, or the coming together of public and private interests to address as a team the needs of humanity. There are many forms of partnership. *The Dignity Doctrine* proposes a way for how we can, through our collective genius and will, attain a more peaceful, just, and humane world. The formula for a more dignified existence begins and ends with us.

My purpose is to challenge you to have an open mind about who you are, where you came from and where you are going—thereby creating a basis for living a happier, healthier, and more fulfilling life. By treating everything in our world, including ourselves, with the utmost reverence, we will in turn lead a dignified existence. To get there we must respect:

- ourselves
- our fellow humans
- the living matter of our Earth
- the physical world including earth, fire, wind, and water
- the nonphysical world—including space, the metaphysical, unknown forces of our universe that affect the earth, collective intelligence, and our consciousness

As the human species there are so many intriguing, unanswered questions about who we are, where we came from, and where we are going. What we all share as humans is the space and time of the present on this place we call Earth. A physical and virtual presence binds us all together. Yet we also seek to understand the depths of the unknown, whether searching for this in space, in the depths of the deep blue ocean, or in the collective intelligence that exists within all living matter. We yearn for truth, understanding, and purpose. Nevertheless, in our pursuit for certainty we often forget that we are bound by a common humanity.

Too often we view other humans as enemies, and out of misguided fear, we perpetuate directly and indirectly a persistent anger and injustice against others. This collective behavior is at odds with humanity and hurts us. The wars we wage outwardly are mostly born from within ourselves. Our madness manifests into turbulent tirades against other people, the "others" we see as different and whom we fear. A more peaceful, just, and humane world begins with each of us. By reconciling within ourselves what it means to be present and connected, aware and conscious, open and willing to understand the world, we can be part of the system of goodness that brings the world and all its people to our fullest potential.

Losing Direction at the Hand of Our Own Moral Compass

Your life and your world are what you make of them. What we choose to see within the world has a direct correlation with our happiness. So too does our willingness and deliberate choice to live life with purpose, conviction, and resolve.

In our lives we often look to external factors and forces to give us positive or negative reinforcement about who we are and what we become. When things do not go our way, it is easier to place frustration or blame on others. This behavior is partly the mind's defense mechanism to protect itself. This reflex is an Achilles heel to our personal growth, health, wellness, and success. Although external forces and factors have a tremendous influence on who we are today, they are by no means the determining factor of who we can be or what we can achieve or become tomorrow.

Our happiness and success in life are entirely dependent upon our worldview (how you see the world), our self-dignity (our self-respect as an individual), and "intentional intuition" (having the grit and courage to take action on our instincts and intuitions).

Humans have a tendency to see and internalize what is happening in the world in the moment, in a small slice of time. We do this for survival. However, when we do this, we do not account for our time in a historical or future context, reinforcing a limited construct of what our minds interpret, and therefore putting boundaries on our capacity to think beyond the moment.

For example, if we objectively looked over the past two hundred years we would see that humanity, in general, has made a remarkable amount of progress across some important domains, including increasing representation of women in business and government, society's greater access to education, medical accomplishments in fighting and curing disease, and great advancements in reducing hunger and poverty and lessening global war and conflict. However, we also have had sustained growth of the human population, which has created tension over natural resource rights and has led to complex and interrelated global concerns of climate change, loss of biodiversity, ecosystem degradation, waste, and pollution.

As humans use the Earth's resources to sustain our living, a fundamental question before us all is whether humans are incrementally bettering our own lives at the accelerated expense of the earth's capacity to enable our very survival. If so, we are then in a self-defeating state of existence. Just as each of us must take care of our mind, body, and spirit to live a healthy and long life, we must also respect the fact that we are the stewards of our communities and the earth. We must take care of ourselves, each other, and the grand planet that provides us with what we currently know as the only habitable place for humans in the universe.

You have likely heard the saying "Don't shit where you eat." I do not mean to be crass or cute here, but humans have to literally and figuratively stop doing this where we eat. By now, we should know better. The truth is that we still get a lot wrong. As a metaphor for treating our own life and all living things with greater respect and appreciation, it is a reminder that it's up to us to educate others and continually cultivate a collective consciousness that has a foundation in mutual respect, peace, love, and dignity.

The simple reality of having a more hopeful, just, equitable, and sustainable world is not complex. But implementing this formula, putting it into practice, is challenging. It requires that each of us understand that our happiness and success is part of a collective whole. In the process, each of us should consider it important for all people to have the opportunity to pursue an enriched life of abundance and success.

At present, the world feels increasingly less hospitable, more irritable, and definitely more irrational. As our shared resources have become constrained, diminished, and degraded, so too has our temperament and respect for one another. In the past decade, fear, frustration, anger, and resentment have compounded our personal and collective existences. Instead of coming from a place of respect and honor, today we seem to be more focused on being right, on winning at the expense of others, and on spiteful revenge. This trending toward a malevolent nature has superseded the moral compass of humanity. In fact, it is as if the polarity of humanity has shifted as many people's moral compasses spin recklessly, seeking direction but never finding their true north.

Humans relate to the here and now. Spending just five minutes trolling social media can bring on a wave of negativity. Or watching a partisan political rant from someone with an opposite view on TV can trounce over you like a tsunami. We should discourage an attraction to a malignant kind of media whose main goal is to whip up our anger and fears with sensational information that exacerbates our anxiety and drains us of any sense of optimism we would normally have for the world. Left unchecked, this results in a kind of mass hysteria that plays out day after day, deepening wounds, perpetuating rifts, and spinning our moral compasses further out of control. Each day we take another hit from a storm of new revelations, events, crises, and catastrophes that impede our ability to reflect on these events to comprehend and reconcile them. we have lost an ability to constructively debate what is true or untrue with any sense of morality or context. One trendy name for this is Trump Derangement Syndrome!

Paying daily attention to hurricanes, wildfires, gender and race inequality, mass shootings, and following tensions over nuclear arms, gun control, human rights abuses, threats of terrorism, and dissension over our corrupt political leaders, makes it really hard to stay optimistic and not feel as if the world if falling apart beneath one's feet. It is true that much of our current affairs feels self-destructive. Although the economy provides the appearance of positive gains and momentum, real predictors of progress and wealth feel as if they are deteriorating. Thus, our mass consumption and internalization of negative news leaves us in a state of continuous assault, fear, and confusion.

Slowly but surely, our dignity is being chipped away each day. When whittled down to nothing, the only thing that remains of the human spirit is a visceral need to survive. We are all potential victims of this phenomenon. People stripped of dignity choose one of two paths, fight or flight, the well-known physiological mechanism that enables us to respond to a harmful threat to our survival. We can then choose to fight off what is threatening us or flee to safety.

The power to regain our dignity and find our true north heading, resides exclusively within ourselves. Fortunately, most of us have the power and human capacity to give and receive love, healing, forgiveness, kindness, and dignity. Each one of us is the steward of our happiness and success in every moment of life.

Life is precious. Do not let anyone tell you differently. For those cynics who believe otherwise perpetrate the loss of human dignity and morality. These perpetrators choose to prolong fear and a negative state of affairs in their personal lives and throughout the world. They are victims of delusion wandering the earth with a broken compass, providing false direction instead of finding their own.

CHOOSING TO FIGHT FEAR

When people lack certainty, they become fearful. Fear is taught and it is learned. Using fear is also a major control over human behavior. Dictators rule by fear. Companies make profits by making people afraid of something. Some religions advance their causes through fear. Fear motivates people to head to the polls but sometimes also keeps them from voting. Fear results in people being taken advantage of. Ultimately, fear leads to indignity.

Fear is a powerful force in our lives, but one that we can proactively counteract, prevent, and reduce. When the human spirit is "broken," it is much easier for perpetrators of fear to seep into our lives. Make no mistake; fear mongers want your soul. They want to control something within your life or your entire being for their political, personal, or financial gain.

Fear is omnipresent, but often it can be controlled and miti- gated. In recent years many "fear factors" have been reinforced across humanity and within specific geographies and sects. For many, fear has been manifested and magnified by current events ranging from terrorism, mass shootings, natural disas- ters, pandemics, nuclear proliferation, hate crimes, human traf- ficking, and social injustices among other calamities. We cannot control every event, outcome, individual, or organization that may influence our lives. We can control however, how we choose to internalize the influences and our reaction to them.

Reflect on your relations among friends, family, cowork- ers, community members, acquaintances, and neighbors. Who among your relations are motivated or controlled by fear? Who among those relations do you feel are your closest confidants or friendly foe?

Whenever you feel fear, take a pause and break that emotion down. What is really going on? Who or what is evoking the emotional response? Evaluate whether the change in your feelings really warranted, or is it a learned behavior from your childhood, deeply rooted in your psyche? Being aware of your feelings and what brings about a change in your energy, your state of being, or emotions is the first step to fighting the influ- ence of fear and the control it can have on your life.

Why Do We Need a Dignity Doctrine? Why Now?

We are living in a time of rapid change and immense challenges. As global population soars so too does our "competition" for life's critical necessities such as clean air, clean water, food, shelter, and clothing. For most of the past century, capitalism has dominated the global business and political landscape. As an economic and political system that favors profit by private owners versus the state, capitalism has created enormous wealth for some, but too often at the expense of many.

Under a capitalistic system of trade and government, financial markets are competitive systems, open to anyone willing to invest and participate. However, capitalism is not a perfect ecosystem that has equal and democratic opportunity. Capitalism, like any social and economic construct, has pros and cons, strengths and weaknesses, waste and inefficiency. Capitalism spurs competition, which can be a powerful leveling agent and force for good, particularly in cultivating resources into values that consumers want. Capitalism can also lead to power structures and unhealthy greed that positions financial profits ahead of the well-being of people and the environment.

This dichotomy and tug-of-war between "free markets," protecting the needs of society, and addressing consumer and citizen interests through the social responsibility of business represents what is called by economists the "social market economy" (SOME). This socioeconomic model combines capitalism with social policies that regulate fair competition in the market and provide safety nets for society to provide what is called a "zone of social, market, political, and creative tension." While not perfect, this zone of tension is what enables capitalism to work. This "zone" is an ever-changing market-based system that provides checks-and-balances on the forces that drive capital markets. In the zone, consumers have always had a voice because they have influenced policy makers through the power of their vote or have influenced business through their individual pocketbook and personal purchasing power.

In recent years, however, consumers have taken on a more prominent role as "activist" consumers and "citizen scientists," choosing to be advocates for change where other institutions have been slow or incapable of acting. In this digital-era of swift information and change, consumers have proven to be well-informed influencers, leveraging social media and other digital tools to magnify their visibility, voice, and influence within the "zone of tension."

As shown in Figure 1, a "zone of tension" exists at the nexus of political, economic, and social influences. This "zone of tension" is were both rational and irrational relations are regularly on display and at play, working for or against specific causes and outcomes. This is the sandbox from which public policy is often initiated, where social movements are spawned, and where new ideas can lead to innovative products or services. This zone is always in flux, always changing with the dynamic evolution of society.

Supported by a greater access to information and the means to share it, consumers and citizens have had a more direct visibility and larger voice in the zone. While in the past citizens may have relied on elected officials or designated authorities to represent their interests before government or business, today citizens are taking a more active role in representing their ideals and toward shaping their future.

Capitalism helps good ideas become innovative solutions, and these can over time become iconic brands and products. Think about contemporary examples of creators of iconic brands and products such as Steve Jobs and the iPhone, Phil Knight and Nike ("Just Do It"), Henry Ford and the Model T, and Levi Strauss and blue jeans. These brilliant business people, their brands and products, and iconic legacy exist within the daily operating realities of capital markets.

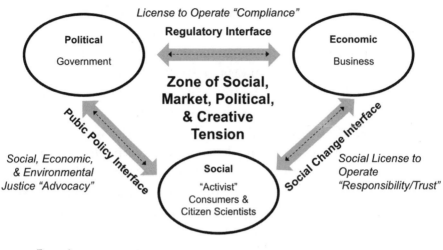

Figure 1

The inventors of these cool products and brands discovered how to fulfill people's unmet needs, the things society longed for or would eventually want and introduced us to their vision of the future through the lens of capitalism. These and thousands of other inventive products and services have captured our imagination and our pocketbooks!

Under a capitalist system of trade and governing, consumers have greater autonomy and control over what types of products and services come into and out of their lives. We have also been artfully convinced to buy products we think we need, some of which we might now lament. Iconic products are those that make the most favorable impression among a majority of customers who willingly choose to identify themselves with a particular brand or product that is their image of high quality and innovation. The iPhone illustrates this phenomenon.

As global population has swiftly increased, society's consumption of natural resources has also increased at an accelerated clip. Capitalism, like ecosystems, is a complex and interrelated system of systems, which is reliant on all of its interdependent parts to remain resilient and functioning.

The world and its resources are a finite system; there is only so much to go around. At least that is what many of us believe. When we view the world as having limits, we place unnecessary limits on our imagination and innovative spirit. It is true that there are functional limits to growth (proven in economic theory, financial markets and within the growth of ecosystems).

The possibility to view the world's resources (as well as our own capacity to thrive) as having distinct limits or having unlimited potential resides with each of us. However, we can acknowledge the facts and truth about system limitations while remaining agile, open, and limitless in our capacity to survive, become sustainable, and attain a better existence. American corporations have awakened to the reality that they too, must change, in order to stay relevant, solvent, innovative, and trusted.

On Monday, August 19, 2019, nearly 200 CEOs of major US corporations issued a joint statement, essentially stating that shareholder value creation is no longer the singular objective of modern business, turning age-old economic theories and prevailing models of business purpose and conduct, including those proposed and developed by the famed Nobel Prize winner, Milton Friedman, on their head.

Founded in 1972, the Business Roundtable (BRT) is a nonprofit association comprised of chief executive officers (CEOs) of major US companies. Notable BTR CEO members include Jeffrey Bezos of Amazon, Tim Cook of Apple, Mary Barra of General Motors, Larry Fink of Blackrock, Inc., Jamie Dimon of JPMorgan Chase & Co., Marillyn Hewson of Lockheed Martin, Ginni Rometty of IBM, and Mark Costa of Eastman Chemical Company. According to BRT, its CEO membership leads companies with "more than 15 million employees and more than $7 trillion in annual revenues."[2]

The mission of BRT is to "promote a thriving US economy and expanded opportunities for all Americans through sound public policies."[3] The BRT CEO members address public policy concerns of corporate governance, diversity and inclusion, education and workforce, energy and environment, infrastructure, innovation, smart regulation, tax and fiscal policy, immigration, health and retirement, technology, and innovation.

In August 2019 the BRT publicly announced that it was redefining the purpose of a corporation as one that would put the interests of employees, customers, suppliers, and communities in which they operate on par with the shareholders. This important announcement published in leading articles in *Fortune* and all major news outlets was led by BRT CEO leaders including Jamie Dimon, Chairman and CEO of JPMorgan & Chase, Co.; Larry Fink, Chairman and CEO of Blackrock, Inc.; and Ginni Rometty, Chairman, President, and CEO of IBM Corporation.

The BRT's 2019 *Statement on the Purpose of a Corporation*[4] is the following:

> Americans deserve an economy that allows each person to succeed through hard work and creativity and to lead a life of meaning and dignity. We believe the free-market system is the best means of generating good jobs, a strong and sustainable economy, innovation, a healthy environment and economic opportunity for all. Businesses play a vital role in the economy by creating jobs, fostering innovation and providing essential goods and services. Businesses make and sell consumer products; manufacture equipment and vehicles; support the national defense; grow and produce food; provide health care; generate and deliver energy; and offer financial, communications and other services that underpin economic growth. While each of our individual companies serves its own corporate purpose, we share a fundamental commitment to all of our stakeholders. We commit to:
>
> - Delivering value to our customers. We will further the tradition of American companies leading the way in meeting or exceeding customer expectations.
>
> - Investing in our employees. This starts with compensating them fairly and providing important benefits. It also includes supporting them through training and

education that help develop new skills for a rapidly changing world. We foster diversity and inclusion, dignity and respect.

- Dealing fairly and ethically with our suppliers. We are dedicated to serving as good partners to the other companies, large and small, that help us meet our missions.

- Supporting the communities in which we work. We respect the people in our communities and protect the environment by embracing sustainable practices across our businesses.

- Generating long-term value for shareholders, who provide the capital that allows companies to invest, grow and innovate. We are committed to transparency and effective engagement with shareholders.

Each of our stakeholders is essential. We commit to deliver value to all of them, for the future success of our companies, our communities and our country.

The words that the BRT members chose to write this carefully written statement are important. The opening sentence, "Americans deserve an economy that allows each person to succeed through hard work and creativity and to lead a life of meaning and dignity," in many ways says a lot about the state of affairs in America and throughout the world.

Jamie Dimon, Chairman and CEO of JPMorgan & Chase, Co. stated, "The American dream is alive, but fraying. . . . Major employers are investing in their workers and communities because they know it is the only way to be successful over the long term. These modernized principles reflect the business community's unwavering commitment to continue to push for an economy that serves all Americans." There are many facets to sustainability, sustainable enterprise, and human dignity.

It seems however, that even a market-based capitalistic economy has its limits, but also is not afraid of evolving so that it, too, can have the opportunity for advancing and sustaining into the future. To attain a more humane, peaceful, just, and sustainable existence humanity must focus its attention on intentional innovation, courageous collaboration, and radical partnerships. This in essence is part of the transformation underway at each of the companies represented by the BRT.

Change Yourself, Change the World

Although many associate change with being a sudden and unexpected event, change is more often a process. It is true that change can be sudden and unexpected, particularly when it comes to a topic I find most people would prefer not to discuss—the event of death.

Most people do not know when they or their loved ones will pass. We do know death always brings about change. And eventually it will happen. The only things we do not know is when and how. In light of this, we should all be able to breathe in a little air of relief. If we come to terms with the inevitability of death, the hardest part is over. What we can then focus our attention on is the hard work of taking full responsibility for life, choosing to live it with a fervor and purpose.

We are here on earth for a fixed amount of time. There is discomfort in not knowing how long we will be alive. However, there is certainty in knowing that the life we live in our physical form has limitations. Knowing this helps us grasp the fragility and preciousness of life. It also helps us focus our energies, love, and attention on the power of living. Death, while we may not know when or how it will occur, is a reality of living, and ideally this should be viewed as a normal life process.

Often experiencing change is only as difficult as our minds want to make it. External factors can impose change (the environment, the media, competitors, economic forces), and internal factors (personal events, community events, events in organizations, etc.) also impose or influence other changes.

There are many responses to change. From a minimalist perspective we can be indifferent (nonresponsive) or accepting of change. When we are accepting of change, we force ourselves to be innovative. Change requires us to think, act, and behave differently than we did before the change. That is why change is uncomfortable. When change feels imposed, we may push back on the change. If the change is inevitable, we may become spiteful and ultimately indifferent. When this happens, change can have a negative impact on individuals and organizations, yielding unintentional outcomes. The model shown in Figure 2 provides a basic example of how humans deal with change. It looks at this through the lens of personal and organizational image (brand) and reputation. More intentional outcomes result when we work to influence change with a sense of innovation and pragmatism. If we succumb to indifference or a status-quo mentality of incrementalism, change can consume us, yielding unintended and unintentional outcomes.

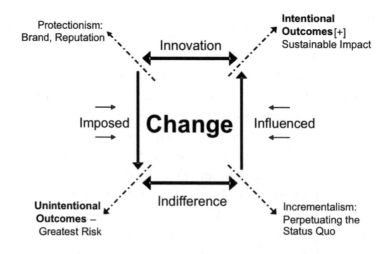

Figure 2

When change is embraced (that is, when people willingly choose to influence change in their behaviors, mindsets, actions, and perceptions) there is a much greater likelihood that intentional and positive outcomes will result. When individuals or organizations do not fully embrace the change or push back against the change this may yield a mindset of either protectionism or incrementalism. The individual and or organizations do only what they have to do to protect themselves until they willingly invest their energies into leading the change and perhaps misguide it.

The one constant any of us can count on is change. When we put up our feet and sink down into the big cozy sofas of our daily lives, we can quickly become complacent and reluctant to change. As we all have experienced, however, change can strike exactly when we least want it to disrupt us. True to form, change sweeps in and rattles our cage, jolting us up from the sofa to stand alert, wide-eyed, and ready to act. How we act in the face of change is what makes all the difference in whether the outcome will be positive or negative.

Change is here; it is at our doorstep, and it is inevitable. The world is calling for each of us, whether already standing alert or still sunk deep into our sofas, to be the change we want to see in the world. Anything and everything about your life has a purpose. You evoke your purpose when and how you choose to be a part of change.

Therein lies dignity. We live our life's highest purpose when we freely and openly choose to be ourselves, ready for action, ready for change, ready for service. Living a life detached from the realities of change is counter to human needs for identity, love, connection, purpose, and growth. Life is about mixing it up in your "zone of creative tension," utilizing your personality and skills to shape the world in a positive way. Anyone can look at their personal struggles or the woes of the world and play the role of a victim to undesired change. Too many of those people play out the status-quo of society day-in and day-out. What you, I, and we need right now, however, is a world that is ready to roll up its sleeves, one that gets off the sofa and tells a world that is increasingly irrational that we need to recalibrate entrenched relationships, challenge convention, and redefine what it means to be human.

Ecology Feels, Every Night and Every Morn

To see a world in a grain of sand
And a heaven in a wild flower,
Holy infinity in the palm of your hand,
And eternity in an hour.

From William Blake's
"Auguries of Innocence,"
published 1863 in *The Pickering Manuscript*

Humans and ecology are intrinsically linked. When nature speaks, humans react or listen. When human behaviors are destructive to nature, we ultimately hurt ourselves. This fundamental truth is not yet entirely lost in society, but it is something that we need to continually respect, seek to understand, and reinforce in all that we are and do.

I recently enjoyed a picnic with my family. We were perched on a small hill overlooking one of New York's gorgeous Finger Lakes, sitting lazily on a blanket and enjoying the splendor of a mid-summer's morning. As I watched my two boys giddily chase each other around, my mind was brought back to my childhood and the sensation of sitting on a green bed of grass, feeling the sunshine warm my face and bones as a cool breeze flowed through the towering maple and elm trees above my head, bringing their leaves to life in a hypnotic dance of happiness. This summer day with my family was no different. Blue skies and big white puffy clouds were the backdrop of sailboats and powerboats skimming the surface of the beautiful lake as we gazed at the surrounding hills and absorbed the serenity. Days like this, like stolen time in a life that moves too fast, are cherished for the peace, joy, and wonder they deliver.

As the laughter of my boys playing freely soothed my soul, I plucked a blade of grass near my bare feet, held it up to my eyes, and inspected it. It seemed like forever since I had sat still long enough to feel grounded and actually touching earth with my hands. When I sat on the lawn as a child, I would pick a blade of grass and run my fingers over it. As pulled through my fingertips, the grass might have felt sharp on its edges, thick and sticky, or think and pliable, all depending upon the random patch that the blade was taken from.

A tactile muscle memory kicked in and I began to recall going through grade school, learning how plants create energy for growth through photosynthesis supported by the water cycle and from the magical geological, biological, and chemical interactions that need to happen in soils to support vegetative life. As a child I was enthralled with earth's dynamic systems and how humans were impacting the world. In elementary school I used to flip through magazines that highlighted recycling and closed-loop systems to capture waste and reuse it for another purpose. In many ways the world made more sense to me as a ten year old than as an adult.

In his September 12, 1962, Rice University speech, famously called the "moon speech," President John F. Kennedy said, "The greater our knowledge increases, the greater our ignorance unfolds."[5] One thing is for certain, the older and presumably more educated and wiser I become, the less I truly know. Intelligence and knowledge are two separate things, like computing capacity and storage. It doesn't matter how much is stored in our brains. If we are not exploring and enriching our lives every day, asking new and brave questions of self and planetary discovery, seeking out truths and challenging our assumptions, well, then, we are not being human, we're just idle robots.

Life on Earth is teaming with intelligence. As humans, we like to believe that we are literally and figuratively at the top of the food chain. When it comes to our intelligence, however, humans still have a long way to go, as there is much we don't know about ourselves, let along the earth's living systems or the vast expanse of the Universe. We are intelligent because we have self-awareness and have the ability to reason. But just because we have those innate qualities that make us human, does not mean we excel at using them, particularly in developing and putting them to use in a productive and humane way. Humans are a paradox; some might say we have split personalities. We have the intelligence and humanistic capacity and capability to create and love. Yet we also wield hatred and destruction in our DNA and through our actions.

Technology is a creation of humans but is also influenced by the dynamic design and operation of Earth's living systems (called biomimicry). Technology serves as a both barrier and an enabler for humans and nature to coexist. Technology and modern life can, if we choose to let it, distance us from nature. If we shroud our every waking moment and daily life in technology, we can become less in touch with the living systems that enable us to live on Earth. Technology can also, however, be an incredible conduit for ecologic awareness, discovery, and awakening.

For example, advanced environmental sensors are being used to monitor subterranean geologic activity as a means to predict earthquakes and volcanic eruptions. Scientists are also using advanced sensors to detect and monitor the migration of chemical contamination in groundwater, hundreds of feet below the earth's surface. Habitat conservationists have used remote imaging and Light Detection and Ranging (LIDAR) to map sensitive ecosystems in the rainforest. Smartphone technologies have been deployed in places like Liberia to enable local communities to monitor and report illegal deforestation activities.[6]

Humans now have the opportunity to explore and engage with the earth's ecology, climate, water, and geologic systems from land, sea, air and space. A wide range of technologies, including Artificial Intelligence (AI), Augmented Reality and Virtual Reality

(AR/VR), blockchain, robotics and autonomous systems, remote sensing and imaging, and enhanced environmental monitoring and analytical tools are enabling humans to experience the earth's natural world in more intimate, scientific, and dynamic ways. With the help of major research universities, NASA, NOAA, and corporations and philanthropies, an interconnected network of sensors and data systems is being put into place that stands to elevate our awareness and understanding of the interrelatedness, fragility, and resiliency of earth's living systems.

Technology can, when designed and deployed within the right framework for achieving good, be a vital link for human-ecologic connectedness and a powerful extension of human consciousness. Technology, particularly AI, opens our five senses to infinite dimensions of human cognition and understanding. With AI, for example, we can begin to predict slight variations in climate, so as to better simulate the impact of sea water rise on coastal communities in Miami, New York, Stockholm, or Malaysia. This kind of analysis is critical for governments to conduct planning for future scenarios, establish risk management strategies, and fashion appropriate resources to prepare people and our infrastructure for changes in weather patterns that will effect our environment.

English poet, painter, and printmaker William Blake famously wrote "to see the world in a grain of sand" as the opening line to "Auguries of Innocence,"[7] which was extracted from one of his notebooks and published in 1863. Blake's use of the word "augury" is defined as a sign or omen, and the poem reads as a series of paradoxes that float between innocence, evil, and corruption.[8] As a young sophomore in college, I had taken European and American literature classes exposing me to the works of Blake, Wordsworth, Yeats, Thoreau, Hawthorne, Joyce, Melville, Whitman, and many others. Each were brilliant with their own characteristic way of envisioning life through words and imagery. Blake's first line of "Auguries of Innocence" is well known, and I often think of it. The earth (and subsequently our solar system and the

Universe) are grand, complex, and filled with paradox, much as Blake eloquently weaved with his words. But we are also as simple, defined, and connected as a grain of sand. Beauty and wonder can be discovered in the tiniest particles of matter and of living things.

Our world in essence, is what we choose to discover, see, and make of it. Good and evil are choices humans make; they are not omnipresent conditions by which life succeeds or fails. Just as humans "feel" things physically, spiritually, and emotionally, so too does the natural world. Ecology coexists with humans. In a perfect system, we nourish and care for each other. We breathe the clean oxygen produced by plants and plants absorb the carbon dioxide we exhale. The relationship between humans and ecology is not so balanced, however. Right now we take and consume more from nature than we conserve and restore. This imbalanced behavior is ultimately self-destructive and, if left unabated, will lead to the collapse of ecosystems and calamity for humans.

I'm reminded of the philosophical question, "If a tree falls in a forest, and no one is around to hear it, does it make a sound?" Renowned philosophers and physicists including Elbert Einstein and Niels Bohr have asked similar renditions of this question. It has been said that Einstein asked Bohr whether he believed the moon did not exist if nobody was looking at it.[9] Bohr's response was that this was a conjecture that could neither be proven or disproved.

Humans perceive the world through our senses (sight, smell, touch, hearing, and taste). These five senses enable us to observe and interpret the natural world so that we can make sense of our surroundings, as well as survive. But is what we perceive through our senses the exclusive boundaries of truth and reality? Is there more than meets the eye? Are we sensing and interpreting the world through the filter of human sensory capabilities and cognition? The answer is yes. There are other plants and animals on Earth that have, for their own survival needs, evolved to have extrasensory abilities compared to us. For example, dogs can hear frequencies of sound beyond the capabilities of our human ears. The long-range vision of eagles and night vision of owls both are by far superior to humans. Bears can detect smells miles away as well as through snow and ice.

Compared to other animals and living organisms, humans have limitations in our sensing capabilities. Our sense of the world is incomplete. It is more restricted and narrower than other living things. However, with our bigger brains and capacity for reasoning and logic, we are able to assimilate the data that comes in from our senses and put that to use to advance ourselves in ways that are seemingly superior to most animals and living organisms.

The human-centric view of the world is of course quite arrogant, since when a tree falls in a forest it does make a sound. The question is dated. What humans have to now ask ourselves is, "If we allow our ego-driven sense of control over ecology to continue to drive our consumptive behaviors, further exacerbating environmental degradation, will we fail the earth (and ourselves) to the point where we won't have the luxury or option of hearing that a tree has fallen and made a sound?" Our philosophy and attitudes about how we interact with all living things represents one of the most significant existential threats to survival.

In fact, humanity has been at a critical juncture in our relationship with our earth for a long time. I don't like writing that sentence because it assumes we are negligent in our ability to understand the big picture. But unfortunately the cold truth is that we are very negligent. We know right from wrong, and we have enough evidence that human-induced climate change is happening. We know our anthropogenic impact on ecology has been destructive to the earth's capacity to renew and rejuvenate itself, limiting our ability to sustain human existence if we don't significantly curb our consumptive behaviors.

Humans have adapted to climate, political, social, economic, and technological changes for thousands of years. Every human being needs oxygen, water, and food to survive. The continuous effective operation of Earth's ecosystems is in every person's best interest. We will continue to adapt, but we also need to rethink how we govern, protect, conserve, retain, and restore ecosystems so that we can continue to sustain life. Furthermore, we need to innovate so that we can mitigate future risks associated with climate change and other existential threats that could be more severe than our best analytical tools and models are predicting.

There is a preponderance of evidence that shows humanity is on the cusp of a new period of awakening and action. Climate change is making, and will continue to make, profound impacts on how society lives, works, plays, and sustains itself. Climate variability will further constrain humanity's access to natural resources, including clean air, water, and food. As a result, the modern age will continue to go through some tough transitions. This will likely result in conflicts over the available natural resources (resource wars). Conversely, humanity could get its act together and discover the power of cultural collaboration. I'm hopeful that we can achieve the latter. So, too, is Eric McLamb, a friend who is a veteran of environmental and entertainment media and who has worked for the media giants Turner Broadcasting System (TBS), CNN, and The Discovery Channel. He says that humanity is anchored by a common "environmental unity."

Mr. McLamb's perspective is pragmatic. We are all interconnected on Earth. Every single one of us, no matter our status of wealth, political affiliation, race, or creed, are already feeling the effects of climate change, whether we realize it or not. We are being squeezed, not only by the clutches of our altering climate, but by the pressure to take matters into our own hands. The next era of evolution for humanity will be marked by significant change. We will be asked, pressured, and finally required to create new constructs of collaboration that challenge our nature and ability to trust each other and what we believe in. However, if we can lead a cooperative effort to find solutions with rational discourse and good relations, we can achieve a more just, peaceful, and sustainable world.

Ecology feels and senses us, just as we feel and sense ecology. The blade of grass that I ran through my fingers has intelligence. Every living organism on Earth is a marker, a clue, a time stamp, a piece of the puzzle, and an embedded code available to us so that we have the building blocks for survival. The resources before us are so much greater than how many years of oil or gas reserves we have left to light up a city.

The ecologic resources on Earth represent a biochemical-geologic road map for the future of humankind. We have all the ingredients for the making of an incredible future. But the kitchen is full of cooks, each wanting to bake their own recipe, and few willing to sit down to talk, listen, compare notes, and innovate together. This requires courage and leadership that the world has never seen. This is the time for us to evolve, spiritually, emotionally, and generationally, toward a more mutual framework of ecologic and environmental unity.

We need to be brave and audacious to change and evolve as we need to and want to and not at the hands of external forces. We need to do this proactively and by our own accord. We need to fight, not among ourselves, but against anything that challenges our dignity and rights and stands in the way of the survival and growth of all of humankind. We can do this because humans exercise free will, the ability to choose our path in life, and our destiny.

It is time for us to stop pitting ourselves against one another. There is so much to learn and so much to do. We must choose to combat with resolve any crisis that can destroy our home here on Earth.

President John F. Kennedy's created a similar call to action in his famous "Space Speech"[10] of 1962 when he stated, "We choose to go to the moon. We choose to go to the moon in this decade and do the other things, not because they are easy, but because they are hard, because that goal will serve to organize and measure the best of our energies and skills, because that challenge is one that we are willing to accept, one we are unwilling to postpone, and one which we intend to win, and the others, too."

My boys have stopped chasing each other. The youngest has a stick and is tracking a carpenter ant as it trots along a sunlit stone wall separating us from the lake. The older brother is next to him. The youngest makes the ant move direction by periodically putting the end of the stick in its path. The ant shifts direction. The ant is persistent, determined. So is the instigator. I intervene and say "leave the ant alone.'" My son replies with a tone, part embarrassment for bothering the ant, and part attitude as if he already knew that the demand was coming from his dad, "okaaay."

Shifting direction is easy. Stopping what we're doing when we inherently know it is wrong is harder. But make no mistake, we are all ultimately accountable. It is our job to intervene, to ask each other to live together, in the grace of each other, to a higher order.

> *The way we see the world shapes the way we treat it. If a mountain is a deity, not a pile of ore; if a river is one of the veins of the land, not potential irrigation water; if a forest is a sacred grove, not timber; if other species are biological kin, not resources; or if the planet is our mother, not an opportunity—then we will treat each other with greater respect. Thus is the challenge, to look at the world from a different perspective.*[11]
> —DAVID SUZUKI

A Convergence of Trust: Moving from Climate Control to Climate Accountability

Climate change. Unfortunately, this phrase has evoked all kinds of tension and raw emotion, at least among skeptics in the United States. However, just saying this politically charged phrase aloud sounds "so 2005." The sheer fact anyone debates climate "change" is ridiculous. Climate has never been static; it has always been in flux. Humans have adapted to climate fluctuations for thousands of years.

In recent years, the #FakeNews movement has challenged scientific, political, and business communities to defend beyond a reasonable doubt that climate change facts, figures, and formulas are legitimate. It is time for us to retire "climate change" as a phrase, much like "sustainability," that is far too passive, political, and polite to reflect the current state of affairs and needs of our communities. It time to accept the truth; we cannot fully control the climate or environment. However, humans are part of a dynamic living system that responds to our influence. We have, within our capacity for knowledge and capability, the means to live very well without negatively affecting the environment and ultimately creating unwanted and undue harm to ourselves.

Global interconnectivity has brought about more awareness and visibility to local and regional concerns than ever before. Seemingly, as the world has become more digitally connected, people have become more engaged and seek truth and understanding of the human condition with its myriad of phenomena, including "climate change" which many do not understand or believe to be true.

Some might argue that a recurrent skepticism in society has grown in-step with the advancement of technology around the world. Taken at face value, a healthy dose of skepticism can be healthy, challenging a status-quo mindset and enabling business and government leaders to remain vigilant and on their toes. However, in recent years a heavy and toxic suspicion or even cynicism has been manifested on social media, in boardrooms, and among the masses. When built up as an unhealthy societal norm, this kind of skepticism breeds misguided judgment, mistrust, anger, and resentment.

Meanwhile, as the people and processes that produce data are scrutinized, visible impacts of a changing climate wreak havoc on humanity. The years 2014 through 2018 were the hottest on record globally. The frequency, severity, and intensity of major climatic events dominated headlines in the past few years have forever changed the lives of millions of people worldwide. Deadly fires, flooding, earthquakes, tsunamis, volcanic eruptions, hurricanes, and other weather and climate events shook and shattered communities all over the world. It is fact that the earth's climate is changing at the hands of human influence. We must get control our actions and behaviors and how we choose to evolve in a world of increasing climate variability.

Politically, we need to move beyond the rhetoric of whether or not climate change is real, what industries are to blame, and who is responsible. It is time to recognize that we are not living in some augmented or virtual reality of normal and haphazard weather phenomena. Rather, we are neck deep in a global climate transformation. There is no escaping the blatantly obvious reality that physical, biological, chemical, climatic, and ecological systems of the earth are undergoing rapid transformation. Make no mistake, humans occupy a planet with finite (albeit renewable and restorative) resources. Some resources have been overconsumed, but we have discovered how to "sustain" others.

Our current quality of life is based on a historical evolution that clearly demonstrates that we will do everything within our power to adapt to the earth's dynamic conditions. One need to look no further than how we heat and cool our homes, workspaces, entertainment facilities, and government buildings in regions as dry and hot as a desert to be as cold as a remote area on top of a mountain. Humans adapt. Using resources from the earth for survival makes sense. It is what we do to survive. No one wants to freeze in the snow or die of dehydration in the sun.

Humans are not content to have simple survival. Our need to survive and to be comfortable and to live where we want on our planet has inspired our ingenuity to enable us to perfect microclimates in our homes, buildings, and communities. We have also transferred our knowledge of climate control to create new environments for indoor agriculture, precision manufacturing, document preservation, and a host of other values we deem important.

Who would not want to swim in a heated pool in a perfectly air-conditioned indoor environment protected from the sun, in Phoenix, LA, Miami, or Dubai?

But in our success to control our climate we have negatively affected the environment with problems of pollution, waste, and other ecologic damages that have come to haunt us. Thus, we have created our own negative feedback loop. As we consume more nonrenewable resources in an unsustainable manner to modify microclimates for our safety, health, comfort, and entertainment, we have inadvertently shifted the burden of climate change into the future and on the next generations.

As we kick the proverbial climate can down the road, we reinforce this negative feedback loop by continuously modifying microclimates. Humanity has created a cycle of negatively reinforcing climate and ecologic degradation. Humans are more intelligent than this. We need to move beyond the capricious phrase "climate change" and focus all of our intellect and energies on climate convergence, the insertion and integration of smart and sustainable technologies that protect, restore, and sustain the earth's natural resources while simultaneously delivering us the climate adaptation and security utilities we have grown to love.

Some pundits have taken the irrational position that the belief that we are in a time of climate change is an argument against our way of life, a rhetoric used to mobilize the masses to take swift action to slay a defiant mythological beast. The beast we seek to slay is omnipresent. Nevertheless, we proceed as if we are at war against our transitioning climate. Our reality is that we are at war with ourselves. The formula for eradicating the local and global impacts of human-induced climate change begin and end with ourselves. We need to look no further than our behaviors, patterns, and trends to recognize that the interconnected systems of life that comprise the planet and sustain our life have been repeatedly bludgeoned by the hammer of humanity.

To address a rapidly altering climate, we need to reassess our basic human wants and needs and the systems and institutions which we continue to perpetuate unsustainably at the expense of overall health and vitality of Earth's living systems (and ultimately ourselves). Climate change is more visible than ever, not only because there are more people with the means to adjust their climate in the moment, but because we've struck the "human control" hammer hard too many times. It is time for humanity to innovate new tools and processes along with new politics and purpose. In the face of a changing weather conditions and temperatures, we can choose to argue among ourselves or converge and innovate.

There is a persistent disconnect about the use of our land. People inherently know that natural resources and ecological systems provide the fuel (energy), the filter (cleaning), and the foundation (backbone) for all living matter, including humans in our systems of water cycling, photosynthesis, carbon sequestration, and so forth). But for far too long we've taken for granted the purpose of our land. It has been largely valued for the services it delivers us as humans. We regarded it as an inert, one-dimensional resource to be exploited for economic gain. We did not realize that our land is not primarily an asset to be economically optimized but is a part of an integrated ecological system we depend on for the clean air, water, nutrition, good health, and well-being that provides our joy and happiness on this planet. By regarding it mainly as a human asset we had decoupled our true reliance on land and the quality of our lives and all beings on Earth.

Today, a child born in an urban area may never have the experience of knowing where their food comes from. They can order food online, eat prepared foods from a local restaurant, or shop at a local grocery store, all without ever having to understand and appreciate the necessary care for land that is required to grow, harvest, prepare, package, and deliver to us fresh, nutritious food each day. We need to reawaken our understanding of the connection between ourselves and the land under our feet. We need to recalibrate our consumer-driven thirst for living with our innate desire to preserve and protect the ground and soil, which we inherently know enriches and sustains our human experience.

Humans have the collective wisdom and intellect to make more informed choices and decisions regarding our shared land and the quality of living we want to have. Together we can address the climate crisis and even regard it as an opportunity to protect and restore our earth and ourselves. The question before us is not whether we are trapped by limited natural, financial, or intellectual resources. Rather, the future and fate of our human condition are a question of whether we have the required moral judgment, leadership, personal accountability, and political will to prevail to solve the crisis.

The climate is changing. Are we also willing to change?

★ ★ ★

PART ONE

Finding Hope and Happiness in an Increasingly Irritable and Irrational World

In his 2008 book *Hot, Flat, and Crowded: Why We Need a Green Revolution—And How It Can Renew America,* Thomas Friedman eloquently summed up the state of the world and global affairs. One needn't look farther than the book's title for us to want to pick up our heads up from our iPhones to see whether Friedman's observations were right on target. Ironically, during the 2007–2008 time frame the world also went through an unprecedented financial crisis. To recap the pain body for full effect, 2008 bore witness to the following top economic calamities, just a sample of what occurred in that year:

1. Bear Stearns bailout
2. Freddie Mac and Fannie Mae bailout
3. Lehman Brothers bankruptcy, triggering a global recession
4. The nationalization of AIG to curb further financial losses
5. Freezing of credit markets
6. End of investment banking
7. Stock market crash

Perhaps if Friedman had published the book a few months later his title might have read, "Hot, Flat, Crowded, Corrupt, and Broke!"

It has been more than a decade since the global financial meltdown of 2008 and the release of Friedman's book. Since that time, there have been many notable global events, societal challenges, and new thought-provoking books that have been published. Friedman's observations of '08 have turned out to be perennial and intensifying. In fact, in the past ten years the world had gotten hotter, flatter, and more crowded:

Hotter World – According to NASA,[12] "seventeen of the 18 warmest years in the 136-year record all have occurred since 2001. The year 2016 ranks as the warm-est year on record."

Flatter World – In 2017 there were more than 1.54 billion smartphones sold worldwide compared to 139 million in 2008, a 1000% increase in less than ten years.[13]

More Crowded World – There are roughly *1 billion more* people on planet earth in 2019 than in 2018. There are 7.7 billion people in the world as of November 2019 compared to 7.6 billion in May 2018. In ten years there was an increase of 10 billion people (in 2008 there were an estimated 6.7 billion).

During this time we've also witnessed more severe, damaging, and fatal natural disasters and storm events; we've seen an increase in domestic mass shootings; there has been a steady increase in the diagnosis of depression and other mental health conditions among our youth,[14] and there has been a swift and tragic increase in deaths related to the overdose of opioids.[15] I'm not (necessarily) trying to draw causality between a hotter, flatter, and more crowded world with higher incidence of social problems and mental health and medical challenges. However, suffice it to say the backdrop of a more congested, digitally distracted, and natural resource-constrained world is not doing us any favors. In the past ten years, the trials and tribulations of being human have only intensified. Humans are resilient.

Over thousands of years of practice, we have cultivated a unique skill and knack for survival. However, although we have had plenty of time for training and trial and error experiments; we have yet to perfect the art of attaining a future where everyone is respected, cared for, and has an equal opportunity to thrive. Our reality is that our world is closing in on us.

We are in a self-imposed pressure cooker that is ready to burst. As intelligent as humans are, we continue to do stupid things. There are many around us who, by their very nature and behavior, are self-absorbed, selfish, and sinister. They care for nothing and nobody but themselves. They justify their existence believing it is within their human right be egocentric. It is within their God-given rights!

This book was not written to challenge or chastise those that choose to live their life according to a code of conduct different from mine. I want to illuminate the simple idea that if we look beyond our selfish needs, we might discover a world filled to the brim with a wealth of love, kindness, happiness, and opportunity. It is up to each of us to find a way to live life with a sense of purpose, passion, dignity, and resolve. I believe each of us is here for a reason. There can be adventure, joy, hope, and humility in discovering that reason.

To get there, you have to look both inside yourself to understand your fears, motivations, needs, and desires. To guarantee your future I believe you have to be willing to decode your past and optimize your present state of being. To accomplish this requires an ability to ground yourself in a way that your mind and consciousness can separate your true self from your ego.

The true value of a human being is determined primarily by the measure and the sense in which he has attained liberation from the self.[16]

—ALBERT EINSTEIN

Manifesting one's purpose can be directly correlated to a massive action of focused service with an intended impact. Your reason for being can be felt through deliberate meditation and mindfulness, but ultimately, it is awakened and put to use by the act of doing. When your true self shines, it's often because you've engaged in a conviction of your purpose for being alive. That only happens when your true self is aligned with your service. Your service can be to your family, community, faith, career, and other individuals or organizations. But what's important is that your good intentions drive the behavior, not what we call our ego.

We are all here on Earth to survive. Yet some of us are positioned much better from birth to survive and live much more freely and fluidly than others. For those of us lucky enough to be born healthy and free, and nourished and loved, let us give thanks for that miracle. For others who from the moment they enter the world are overwhelmed with disease or endangered by oppression and fighting for dear life for their survival, let's pray they can be with us another hour, day, month, or year and improve their condition. There is no time for guilt, fear, anger, or passing blame for our human condition. Life is far too precious and fickle for any of us to waste time or energy worrying about circumstance outside of our control. But for those of us who have the capacity within our heart, mind, and body to be of help to our fellow beings, let us exercise that opportunity whenever we can. For we can, through service to others, enrich their lives as well as our own.

1

The Politicization of Dignity

After the end of World War II, the United Nations (UN) came into being to "bring peace to all nations of the world." Then First Lady of the United States, Mrs. Eleanor Roosevelt[17] (wife of President Franklin D. Roosevelt), headed a special committee of dignitaries who wrote one of the UN's early declarations called the Universal Declaration of Human Rights.[18] This declaration contains 30 statements that spell out a global accord for ruling nations by the UN's 192-member General Assembly of nations:

> Where, after all, do universal human rights begin? In small places, close to home—so close and so small that they cannot be seen on any maps of the world. Yet they are the world of the individual person; the neighborhood he lives in; the school or college he attends; the factory, farm or office where he works. Such are the places where every man, woman, and child seeks equal justice, equal opportunity, equal dignity without discrimination. Unless these rights have meaning there, they have little meaning anywhere. Without concerted citizen action to uphold them close to home, we shall look in vain for progress in the larger world.[19]

—Eleanor Roosevelt, wife of US President Franklin D. Roosevelt, and Chair of the United Nations Commission that wrote the Universal Declaration of Human Rights in 1948

United Nations 30 Articles [abbreviated] of a Universal Declaration of Human Rights to be Followed by all Countries	
Article 1	Right to Equality
Article 2	Freedom from Discrimination
Article 3	Right to Life, Liberty, Personal Security
Article 4	Freedom from Slavery
Article 5	Freedom from Torture and Degrading Treatment
Article 6	Right to Recognition as a Person before the Law
Article 7	Right to Equality before the Law
Article 8	Right to Remedy by Competent Tribunal
Article 9	Freedom from Arbitrary Arrest and Exile
Article 10	Right to Fair Public Hearing
Article 11	Right to be Considered Innocent until Proven Guilty
Article 12	Freedom from Interference with Privacy, Family, Home and Correspondence
Article 13	Right to Free Movement in and out of the Country
Article 14	Right to Asylum in other Countries from Persecution
Article 15	Right to a Nationality and the Freedom to Change It
Article 16	Right to Marriage and Family
Article 17	Right to Own Property
Article 18	Freedom of Belief and Religion
Article 19	Freedom of Opinion and Information
Article 20	Right of Peaceful Assembly and Association
Article 21	Right to Participate in Government and in Free Elections
Article 22	Freedom of Opinion and Information
Article 23	Right to Social Security
Article 24	Right to Desirable Work and to Join Trade Unions
Article 25	Right to Adequate Living Standard
Article 26	Right to Education
Article 27	Right to Participate in the Cultural Life of Community
Article 28	Right to a Social Order that Articulates this Document
Article 29	Community Duties Essential to Free and Full Development
Article 30	Freedom from State or Personal Interference in the above Rights

SOURCE: University of Minnesota Human Rights Resource Center
http://hrlibrary.umn.edu/edumat/hreduseries/hereandnow/Part-5/8_udhr-abbr.htm

Human Rights in Our Era

As far as the UN's Universal Declaration of Human Rights, abuse remains rampant throughout many societies. This is an ugly reality for humanity. When someone exploits another human being against their will, without their knowledge or consent, in order to gain an advantage (such as behavior benefiting someone's political, economic, financial, professional, sexual, and labor needs or for the purpose of any other personal benefit), this is abuse.

Although abuse is often rooted in hatred, bigotry, racism, and sexism, it does not discriminate about who is impacted. Whether old, young, rich, poor, white, black, man or woman—abuse can affect anyone. Abuse is atrocious and can take many forms. It can be physical, emotional, spiritual, financial, sexual, and psychological. It can also be outlandish and blatant or subtle and silent.

Although abuse can be manifested in many forms, it is often subject to broader human rights issues such as social inequality, racial discrimination, a system of slavery, and other persecution and torture based on religion or nationality. As troubling as abuse is, the politicization of abused individuals or groups of peoples is even more disturbing. Unfortunately, that is exactly what continues to occur in the United States and in other countries of the world when economic, social, religious, environmental, or political factions and issues prolong human rights abuses.

In 2018 the Trump administration instituted a "zero tolerance" policy for enforcing border crossings along the southwest board of the United States and Mexico. As a means to deter illegal crossings, the administration put into place a process to separate migrant children from their parents at the US-Mexico border. This arcane and cruel policy resulted in more than 2,300 children separated from their parents over just a few months' time.

Between April and July 2018, the separation issue was widely politicized, pitting the Trump administration, Republicans, and Democrats against each other in a tug-of-war fight over immigration policy and human right. As public outcry in the United States and abroad magnified, it began to weigh down on the Trump administration. Two administration appointees working to defend their highly conservative stance on separation addressed the press, public, and Congress by issuing the following statements:

> On June 14, 2018 US Attorney General Jeff Sessions defended the Trump administration policy by quoting the Biblical passage from Apostle Paul's epistle to the Romans, stating, "I would cite you the Apostle Paul and his clear and wise command in Romans 13, to obey the laws of government because God has ordained them for the purpose of order . . . orderly and lawful processes are good in themselves and protect the weak and lawful."[20]

> On June 18, 2018 US Homeland Secretary Kirstjen Nielsen stated the Trump administration "will not apologize" for separating families, because, "we have to do our job . . . we will not apologize for doing our job . . . the administration has a simple message—if you cross the border illegally, we will prosecute you."[21]

Meanwhile, thousands of children were detained in Customs and Border Protection facilities and immigrant shelters including "tent camps." By June 26, 2018, a federal judge in California ordered US immigration authorities to reunite children and families on the border within 30 days, and for children younger than five years of age, the reunification was to occur within 14 days.

Now, try to remove, just for a moment, your personal opinion on immigration policy, border security, human and drug trafficking, and any other issue or excuse you want to put out in front of this ugly American event. Anyone who has a pulse, whether you have children or not, inherently knows how horrifying it is to separate children from their parents. Imagine children as young as newborns and infants separated from their mothers, particularly under the pretense and uncertain circumstances in which this abhorrent act occurred. Now put yourself in the shoes of a refugee trying to reach a "promised land" of freedom and opportunity only to realize a proverbial wall is the worst of your worries. Everything you have traveled and fought for, the promise of opportunity for your children and family, ripped apart and divided.

These individuals want freedom so badly that they are willing to risk their family's prosecution, separation, and detainment. Yet, here we are, 244 years after the United States became a nation brought together by a group of foreign outsiders, witnessing America the great willfully separate children and families under a rule of law. Most people know that these events were not an act of legal authority or national security—this was an act of outright politics, administrative bullying, and abuse of human rights.

America, built upon a foundation of human rights, democracy, and independence, was showing the world that it does not fall in line with the ideals that actually make this country great. For most Americans, myself included, the politicizing of migrant children to make a point is highly reprehensible. Trump and his administration's behavior do not represent the values of this country or our doctrine and commitment to other peoples of the world.

Just as Mrs. Eleanor Roosevelt said before the UN in 1948, "concerted citizen action" is required for a free, just, peaceful world. While human rights abuses fall victim to political football, it is up to each of us, acting within our rights and freedoms, to stand up for those that are unintentionally or knowingly victimized and oppressed during their justified pursuit of dignity and freedom.

Friends, if you want freedom, you must be willing to stand up for what is right and fight for it. That fight happens every day all around the world. Freedom is not a given; it is something that you have to actively participate in. When human rights abuses happen right before our eyes, we have a choice. We can sit idly by or we can jump in, roll up our sleeves, use our intellect and our voices, and stand for what is just and right. Make no mistake, when the rights of other humans are abused, your rights are also abused. It is ill-advised to be complacent or apathetic to the abuse of others human rights. If we do not come together to fight for others rights when they are in need, we might just find that in the not so distant future we are the subject of the late "Breaking News" story.

We have a serious problem with our branding image and reputation in America. Mrs. Roosevelt declared that people seek to find, protect, and serve small places, close to home, where every *"man, woman, and child seeks equal justice, equal opportunity, equal dignity without discrimination."* To this point, our history and rich heritage as a nation speaks of a promised land where personal freedom continues to be fought for, where if you work hard you can achieve great things. That place is very much real; it is not a mythical country of legends, fantasy, or folklore.

However, the brand of freedom many people thirst for, and are willing to put themselves in harm's way to access, is not the same brand that many American's wear on their sleeve. It seems many of the lucky few hundred million American citizens that call the United States home from the circumstance of their birth need to be reminded just how hard fought the winning our collective freedoms have been.

America is a multifaceted nation, a diverse and vast country of enormous irony and dichotomy. Extreme wealth coexists with extreme poverty. Education and health care are accessible, but not all school districts, health-care clinics, hospitals or communities have equitable distribution of financial resources to support them. A range of social issues continues to persist within American society, draining our emotional and economic resources. They include racism, illiteracy, poverty, unemployment, gender inequality, alcoholism, drug abuse, political corruption, child labor, child abuse, lack of affordable housing, civil rights violations, inadequate education opportunities, pollution, immigration problems, homelessness, bullying, need of health-care reform and gun control, breaches of privacy, and many others. Dignity is essential to helping address and solve every single one of these unrelenting social problems.

America is also a technology unicorn, akin to startup stars out of Silicon Valley. The country grew up very fast and within a few hundred years came to be a world phenomenon of a military, economic, political, and cultural powerhouse. Much of this was accomplished on the backs of what were human rights abuses, taking advantage of immigrants, enslaving people, and stealing the land out from beneath the feet of Indigenous peoples. Along the way, the United States developed a cultural consciousness and became the world's protector of democracy and freedom.

Then the events of September 11, 2001, shook Americans to their core. The horrific events of 9/11 were an extremely emotional modern-day turning point for American culture. Since then, more cynicism, hatred, insular thinking, and protectionism has seemed to manifest itself within the country, perpetuating many social needs and problems. It seems we have not fully healed from the events of 9/11.

Directly following the attacks on September 11th, 2001, the United States government, military, and intelligence communities took swift action. Taking action is what we know how to do very well. When American freedom and democracy are threatened, we rise up to the challenge and take immediate action. Our psyche is such that we cannot ever let our guard down. While most citizens of the United States rally and rise against atrocities and serve in times of significant need, we often do not internalize the plight of freedoms that may be slowly slipping from our grasp. If an event, issue, or concern does not have an immediate infringement on our personal freedom, we tend to be passive, over analytical, and ambivalent. When we are touched personally, however, watch the hell out.

This draws the question, when it comes down to living up to our brand promise and purpose, that is, what it means to be a citizen of our country. Have Americans become too passive (dare I say even lazy)? I believe there is plenty of proof that we have. Whether we are easily entertained by a president, the likes and behaviors we have never experienced before, or more comfortable on the sidelines in our cozy couch watching "Breaking News," we seem to have become a little forgetful about what we have been through together as a people in our nation's history.

Since the 2016 presidential election I have heard so many people including "independent" journalists, political wonks, and grocery store clerks say things like, "There is no precedent for the behavior of Trump . . . no one like him has ever been president before . . . we just don't even know how to react to this . . . he tweets about things constantly . . . he is unhinged." If you uncritically listen to the opinions of other people long-enough you begin to believe what they are saying. Trump happens to have a gift, possibly better than his predecessors did, for creating a constant noise machine of illusion, distraction, and perception, with all of the attention focused on himself.

I have found that many Americans, for a period, were simply awestruck by what would come out of the president's mouth or what would be tweeted next. If Howard Stern is the "shock jock" of radio and John Gotti the "Teflon Don" of the Mafia, then Trump might be "BOTUS," an acronym for Bully of the United States, reflecting both his personality and obsession with using Twitter to attack those who criticize him, and the fact that he appears to live his life through the lens of public perception and ratings like a game show host. For someone who despises the media, Trump certainly wants the news story to be always about him. Unfortunately, the media and public have their reasons for complying with this.

Most Americans are innocent bystanders watching current events play out. These days Trump is usually the main character and serves the roles of production hands, writers, musicians, and other actors. Some have paid to watch this production, and he wants all of us sitting eagerly in our chairs with our snacks, utterly captivated. Instead of feeding the beast, it would be best if we all silenced our phones and streaming media for some moments of silence. Imagine that— silence! What we might find is that we are a whole lot happier and less frustrated. Further, we might discover that through all of the noise and chatter of the Trump production, we have allowed ourselves to be too distracted. We have taken our eyes off what is important and spent too many hours waiting for "what could possibly happen next." Well, enough wasted time already. It is time to move beyond the hype, glitz, dysfunction, and noise and take action to create a better world for ourselves and our family.

The time is now to shake ourselves free from the shackles of shock and daily desensitization that we call the media. The United States is beautiful and is a great place here and now. "You, me, and we" make it so. So let us do our part—every single last one of us—to make our individual and collective lives as dignified as possible; we can then stand up for all that we are, all that we believe in, and hope for all of those who seek refuge and opportunity in this great land we call America.

How to Live and Thrive in a World Torn Between Scarcity and Abundance

After *The Sustainability Generation* was published, I spent a lot of time speaking before a diversity of corporate, college, and community audiences. As much as it was a pleasure to be asked to speak about the inspiration and thesis of *The Sustainability Generation*, I got the most out of engaging individuals and audiences in conversations about their personal views of sustainability. Whether I spoke before 40 scholars at a private university, 40 local community members, or 40 leaders of a major corporation, I began to observe and catalogue similar viewpoints and perceptions people had about sustainability. What I learned is that the vast majority of people think about sustainability as a limiting experience. That is, in order to pursue and attain sustainability, you must give something up.

For example, to get better fuel economy and lower emissions you have to drive a "lesser car"—a vehicle that would be smaller and lighter in size, propelled by a less powerful engine, and delivering a driving experience that was quite boring. If you have ever had the opportunity to drive a Tesla Model X, you know that alternative forms of climate-friendly propulsion systems are anything but boring!

It is interesting to talk with people about their "love affair" with products like cars and smartphones. The way we have personalized consumer products is fascinating and alarming. Many people put a great deal of credence into the relationship they have with their cars, phones, and houses, valuing them as an extension of their identity.

In the case of transportation, ultimately what we need is *mobility*, the ability to physically get ourselves from point A to point B and back to point A efficiently and safely as quickly as possible. The solution for achieving that can be as rugged as gargantuan as a Hummer or as frugal as a Fiat. The need can also be achieved by motorcycle, train, plane, bus, or an autonomous self-driving vehicle. These options range in style, affordability as far price, and in their fuel (energy) consumption, environmental impact, social acceptance or stigma, safety, security, speed, comfort, and other parameters. The need for transportation can be reasonably attained by technology resources and systems we have today.

Right now, Americans place a heavy emphasis on cars, how they drive, what they look like, and what we look like driving them. With that emphasis in mind, the basic utility of getting where we want to go is delivered at a sustainability premium compared to other options. Today, we engineer and manufacture cars to be fully immersive technological and mobility experiences. Welcome to the era of mobility as a service. In this new model of transportation, consumers pay not only for mobility (the basis utility of moving us from point A to point B) but also for delivering premium sound for entertainment as we drive, unparalleled safety, and a host of other features that compensate for driver errors—leading us to a future where we won't even have to be bothered with the actual driving.

In the future the car-bot will be preprogrammed to take us where we need to be, when we need to be there, and with our desired comfort needs and audio and entertainment settings customized for us. Forget about daydreaming out the window. The future of personalized mobility will transform the time you now spend in between point A and B into whatever kind of event you want it to be. The future of mobility will physically move us where we want to go efficiently and safety, and it will also transport our minds, elevate our moods, and deliver us a transformative cognitive experience as well.

Society is on the cusp of a new cultural, technological, and industrial revolution. In the coming decade we will be profoundly swept up in the full immersive experience of technology in ways that far exceed gaming, watching television, or engaging in social media. Our lives will be transformed by products that communicate with each other, absent our involvement. We will be the first generation to reconcile the rights of humans as we establish rights for robots. We will also be the first generation to deal with dooms-day scenarios around a slew of science, technology, and associated risks ranging from augmented and virtual reality (AR/VR), artificial intelligence (AI), genomics and genetic engineering, information security and privacy, and bio-engineering to asymmetric weaponry and warfare. What once read like a science fiction novel will become our new normal, a world where technology is precariously dangling out ahead of humanity's capacity to fully vet and grasp the nuance of the ethical, social, legal, and moral requirements and impacts of the "new" technologies.

This rapid ascension of a technocratic society will yield a new age of social, ethical, economic, and environmental challenges we have never had to contend with before and likely also give us the opportunities to solve them. Thus our individual notion of what "sustainability" should mean and look like will be increasingly be drawn into question.

There is a burgeoning tension in society. It is between political elites and technologists and between wealthy corporate elites and the working class, those that have been forgotten and those that simply are not even recognized as part of society. If we continue down the path of swift technological change absent of a strong moral compass to guide human evolution appropriately, we stand to lose ourselves to an intelligence that we created but cannot control. There is irony in this because ever since we learned to transform our existence, humans have continually pursued methods for manipulating the world around us to conform to our needs.

Although we have never fully controlled the weather, we have been successful at shaping the environment. Look no further than the cityscape or suburban areas and countryside around you. The roads, tunnels, bridges, houses, buildings, shopping centers, eateries, schools, and hospitals all exist at the hand of humanity. We have dramatically transformed the earth, putting a firm imprint of our existence on the face of this rock we call home. We have literally moved mountains, drained and diverted waterways, and turned deserts into an oasis just to meet our needs. Some of this alteration occurred to enable our survival. However, make no mistake. Humans exert sheer force to seek control over our landscapes.

We slice, carve, nip, and tuck the earth as if we are giving it a constant facial makeover, never quite satisfied or pleased with how it is aging. Our desire to transform and reface the earth is not solely the pursuit of vanity. Over the course of millennia, we have come to better understand, value, and respect the symbiotic relationship we have with our planet. We know, inherently and in practical terms, that our pollution and waste is damaging to the earth's life-giving natural systems and ecosystems. We understand that if we create, stimulate, and accelerate limiting factors and feedback loops within Earth's ecosystem we will ultimately become the recipient of its limitations as well.

Today our extreme weather events, water pollution, and problems of resource scarcity are intensifying at a rate that severely challenges our ability to respond. As global population continues to rise, so too does the threat of more significant life-threatening impacts associated with natural and man-made disasters from extreme weather events that result in the scarcity of food and water that leads to hunger and economic distress. How we choose to inhabit and shape Earth, continues to foster negative feedback loops at a scale, reach, and impact that we can barely measure, let alone comprehend.

All around us there is evidence in both our natural and man-made infrastructure and technologies that has shifted the human-centric sense of having control over our environment. The signs are all around us. Our challenges with poverty, hunger, pollution, resource scarcity, and ecologic collapse are all symptoms of our daily relationship with each other and our planet. Our technological innovations are also demonstrations of our desire and need to adapt to change by modifying scientific solutions to guarantee our survival.

Take industrial agriculture, for instance. A century ago, we worked to mechanize production on the farm to provide food more efficiently and cost effectively to hungry mouths around the world. In less than one century, we have shifted from manipulating how we industrialize crop harvesting to manipulating the science of how the agriculture commodity is grown from the start. Knowing that weather events have become more erratic and that the growing seasons can only yield so much profit, scientists have genetically modified seeds to produce crops that are more resilient to drought and disease and which can grow faster and yield more food.

There are benefits and tradeoffs from this manipulation of nature and natural ecosystems, but the key take-away is that humans are at a point of critical decision-making. Our Earth has actively signaled to us that it is overtaxed from our negative influences. We are not living in harmony with our planet and need to address our mindset and values—and our true purpose for being. To avoid falling victim to a rapidly changing climate and environment, we went "all-in" at full steam to reengineer a world that will give us what we need when we want it. There is a God-like complex in this behavior, one that environmental ethicists and philosophers have researched and examined for years. There is also a moral obligation in all that we do as individuals, families, communities, and humans, during our time on Earth. But our number-one objective, rooted deep in our subconscious and made transparent through our conscious behaviors, is simply to survive.

We have greater scientific knowledge and technological capability than previous generations and a greater understanding of earth's natural processes and our impact on climate change and environmental degradation. We have better tools and resources to prevent further ecological destruction and restore existing, ecologic damage. The question is whether we have the personal and political will and conviction to utilize our knowledge and resources for this purpose.

2

The Irrational Irony of Life and Hardening of Humanity

If all living things are ultimately interconnected at some level (ecological, biological, metaphysical, philosophical, and so forth), then why is life so unbalanced, unfair, and unreasonable? Life is a paradox, a sarcastic sitcom of illogical contrasts. Consider the everyday disparities that plague even the most "free" and "wealthy" of nations because a portion of their population struggles with basic survival from a lack of adequate water, food, shelter, and adequate clothing. The conflicts of interest impeding solutions to this come from many directions of opposing values. Often major differences in our ideologies and values are caused by disagreements about the following:

- Civil Society: Militarization and Privatization of Schools vs. Access to Free and Public Education

- Economics: Haves vs. Have-Nots and Rich vs. Poor vs. Middle Class vs. Upper Class (the 2 percent, etc.)

- Politics: Democrat vs. Republican vs. Independent and other parties

- Religion: Christianity vs. Islam vs. Buddhism vs. Atheism, and so forth.

- Health and Technology: Access vs. Cost vs. Affordability vs. Privacy.

- Our Environment: Equity and Justice vs. Open/Accessible Public Lands and the Commons vs. Privatization of Resources

In March of 2018, I was on business travel to New York City. The trip was on the eve of a larger Nor'easter that was pushing up the east coast. Weather forecasters were projecting five to ten inches of wet heavy snow to blanket the city within a twelve to fifteen-hour period. Although the prediction was severe, the day prior to the storm was beautiful. I walked in between business meetings around Park Ave., Madison Ave., and took a brief stroll through Central Park.

New York is real-life in constant motion. If you stopped at any given intersection, took a picture and examined the image, you would bear witness to every one of the seven major human emotions being exhibited by the people captured in the moment: anger, contempt, fear, disgust, happiness, sadness, and surprise. New York, famously the city that never sleeps, includes more than 8.5 million people on roughly 300 square miles of land. It cannot help but evoke raw emotion. Emotion yields reaction and action.

In recent years there has been a "hardening of humanity" brought on by a constant angst and the assault of horrifying and over sensationalized events and news. The mass consumption of negative events has led to a mass desensitization of people. At face value, I do not believe we are less caring, feeling, or loving—but I do frequently sense that people have become numb to everyday atrocities right before their eyes. Let me explain.

As I walked the streets of Manhattan, a stark contrast revealed itself around every corner. Extreme wealth mixed with crushing poverty and helplessness. Panhandlers were asking for spare change from high-fashion flaunters and money brokers. I walked past Trump Tower amid a sea of diverse faces and all walks of life. It was right there, looking up at a tower of dark glass, that I could not help thinking about the deep and widening chasm that exists in America. The gap that exists and which continues to grow is not only between rich and poor. The gap is in our own capacity to demonstrate simple kindness and care for fellow humans, no matter who they are, where they came from, what they look like, or what they choose to believe or worship.

From an early age we are made to either respect and admire great power or to loath and fear it. A shiny black tower casts a long shadow over America. Nevertheless, we can choose to be consumed by the shadow, or to walk (if not run) away from it. I turned a corner to walk a few blocks to Lexington Ave. It was on Lexington Ave., I had been told by a local, where I could find some eateries and convenience stores. The advice proved on-point, as I was craving pizza and discovered a quaint place with a perfect slice. I chose to eat inside the small establishment, absorbing the eclectic ambiance of New York that seeped in from the street and oozed out of the hot pizza oven of the establishment. I ate my slice in silence, taking in the ambient sounds and observing the sights from the street. After a long day of business, the moment felt like a small reward. Although I was but one more person in a fast-paced city of more than 8.5 million, the simplicity of just being present with a slice of pie amidst all of the hustle and bustle brought a sense of peace. I took my time eating, more so than normal. After finishing the pizza slice, I threw out my paper plate and napkins and proceeded out the front door. I turned slightly to the man behind the counter and gave a head nod and said thank you. He said, "Thank you and have a good night," in reply. The trivial exchange somehow felt just right—as if there were a quiet universal recognition of mutual gratefulness—for my belly being filled and for the establishment to have yet another satisfied customer.

After eating, I began my walk back to the hotel. As I walked down a side street, I saw an elderly woman walking alone in front of me. She had a cane to steady her stride. The woman was dressed very nicely, and she seemed content in moving right along the sidewalk at a reasonable clip. The sun had set and the street was darker now. At first I thought how sad it was that she was walking alone. Then I also felt a positive energy and considered how awesome it was that this woman, who must have been at least in her eighties, was out and about doing her thing. I walked around her and found myself looking down at the ground. I noticed another elderly woman covered in a blanket, eyes closed, sitting against a building. The woman on the ground clearly was homeless and appeared even older than the woman I had just walked past.

I then walked up behind a couple who were out with their dog. They too had just passed by both of the women. When I walked by the homeless woman, there was a split second when I hesitated. Why was this dear old woman alone on the street on the eve of a major snow event, covered with just a blanket? Would she find shelter? Did she need help? Would someone help her? Should I help her? Why do some people take kindlier to a stranded dog or cat than a human being? Why do I, or anyone for that matter, hesitate to help another human in need? And what could I realistically do to help her? These and a dozen or so other questions and thoughts rapidly popping in and out of my mind.

But I kept walking. I rationalized my response to the woman on the ground. She would find shelter. Someone else would also see her. Someone else would help her. But what if no one did? What if I were the only person among 8.5 million in NYC who saw this woman for what she was, a human in need of someone, anyone, to influence the fate of her condition? Yet, like hundreds if not thousands of others, I chose to keep walking by.

This all too real scenario is in front of each of us in some form or another. We all go through life thinking and behaving as if there will be someone else to arrive, to pick up the pieces, to clean up the mess, to care for another human. We procrastinate and put things off another day . . . we deflect responsibility and push the "burden" to other people. At what point do we demonstrate concern, care, and compassion? When your time of need arises, and it will eventually, will someone come to your aid or will they walk on by, content after just having had a satisfying and peaceful meal? I am far from perfect and have had many instances in my life where I have passed up the chance to help a fellow human being. I have also had moments where I have quietly gone out of my way to support someone in need. Each day we all have an opportunity to contribute to bettering the world in small and significant ways.

If we let the shadow of the proverbial tower consume us with anxiety and harden our capacity to feel and love, we will never step aside and into the light to see the world differently. It is up to all of us to break free from the shadows that prevent us from seeing the world as a place of understanding, compassion, hope, and promise—and not as something to fear.

Can Humanity Be "Left to Its Own Devices?"

Social Media Needs a New Source Code

For all the great things technology has made possible for humanity, it has simultaneously amplified some of our less favorable social and personal idiosyncrasies. Powered by an iPhone or Android device, anyone can have an ear and microphone to the world. The data and information we choose to see and hear, however, mutates several times over before we actually receive it, interpret it, and decipher it as having value, meaning, or purpose for our lives. Technology enables and celebrates our existence; it also shapes and distorts our reality.

For example, we willingly self-selected what we choose to consume by way of digital delivery. Social media platforms shape our "user experience" by using machine learning and artificial intelligence (AI) to direct content (data, pictures, video, narratives, retail sales, etc.) that we tend to search for and self-direct ourselves to observe. In a democratic society, this is fraught with challenge; hence our government's investigations concluded that the Russians interfered with the United States presidential elections of 2016 via Facebook and other media influences.

When the content that reaches our screens is a distortion of what is actually happening in the world, we no longer have a democratic society. Whether we are willing to accept this truth or not, we are at that point in social history. We are literally, as the saying goes, "left to our own devices" to decode truth from fiction. Although all of us would like to believe we are relatively well-informed, not easily swayed or manipulated, and are critical thinkers, we don't have the skill set to analyze every bit and byte of data that streams into our handhelds or homes.

Therefore, we filter. We make selections based upon our inherent judgment of values, morality, quality, and honesty to deem what is credible content. Our antenna to the world fixates on what we give our attention and time to. To filter truth from falsehoods requires us to be highly informed on the issues of the day. We need to be vigilant, proactive, and continually conscious of events in the world that's physically attainable and right in front of us. We also need to understand the increasingly relentless world that operates autonomously and out of sight—the one powered by AI and robots programmed to mine our personal data for the purpose of guiding our decisions and influencing our behavior.

There has never been a time in history when so many humans can be directly or indirectly instantaneously connected or disconnected from each other. To be complacent or ambivalent about this time of unremitting technological data-driven influence on our lives would be catastrophic to democracy and human dignity. Technology and all that can be manifested from data information on many platforms, including the use of cloud computing, machine learning, AI, and virtual and augmented reality (VR/AR) has become an entirely new ecosystem that humanity relies on. Just as we depend on the natural world and ecological ecosystems to sustain life with clean water, air, food and energy, we have created a technological ecosystem that is "too big to fail."

As technology seeped, flowed, and then poured into our daily lives, it resulted in small, steady, and then constant changes in how we perceive ourselves in an interconnected world. To be clear, we fell victim to the allure of instant and perpetual fame. Social media and other shiny objects in digital space filled a void in our lives for getting attention. Suddenly we could all have a voice and let our inner rock star, comedian, or writer shine through.

YouTube has made overnight sensations out of every-day, regular people. We are all attracted to positive energy. Social media at its best empowers people to share their positive energy. However, it also breeds and feeds off people who have negative energy and who choose to use social media platforms as an outlet to vent themselves or bully people.

In 2017 two UK organizations, the Royal Society for Public Health and the Young Health Movement, collaborated on a study of 1,479 young people, asking them to rate the impact of the five largest social media platforms on 14 distinct criteria comprising their health and well-being. The surveyed youth answered questions on how the social media platforms affected their sleep, anxiety, depression, and self-identity and their experiences of bullying, negative feelings about body image, loneliness, and fear of missing out (FOMO), among other measures. The survey found that youth between 14 to 24 years old had increased feelings of inadequacy and anxiety from regular use of social platforms including Instagram, Facebook, Snapchat, and Twitter.[22] Young people cited that body shaming, bullying, and hostile comments were typical and escalated their feelings of depression, anxiety, and inadequacy.

In the spring of 2018, Twitter CEO Jack Dorsey tweeted , "We have witnessed abuse, harassment, troll armies, manipulation through bots and human-coordination, misinformation campaigns, and increasingly divisive echo chambers. We aren't proud of how people have taken advantage of our service, or our inability to address it fast enough."[23] [11:33 am–Mar. 1, 2018–San Francisco, CA]

Dorsey then followed up tweeting, "Why? We love instant, public, global messaging and conversation. It's what Twitter is and it's why we're here. But we didn't fully predict or understand the real-world negative consequences. We acknowledge that now, and are determined to find holistic and fair solutions." [11:33 am–Mar. 1, 2018–San Francisco, CA]

Then Dorsey announced that the Twitter organization would, from that point forward, seek to measure and understand the "health" of conversations on their platform.

Social media amplifies the human condition. It provides us the means to share our thoughts with the world, relatively openly and freely. Social media is like a drug. It simultaneously feeds our ego, alters our mood, allow us to escape to another realm, and provides us a (false] sense of power and control. Like a drug, social media augments our reality and brings to the surface those emotions, feelings, and behaviors that are usually tempered.

Moreover, like being under the influence of a drug, social media also makes us feel protected—as if we are invincible (and invisible] to the world. Hiding, lurking, creeping behind a cloak of code, we wear our emotions on our sleeves as we post our woes, feelings, opinions, and epiphanies about our life, friendships, lovers, and families for the world to see. I do not believe we can fully assess what the net impact of this age of mass sharing has had on individuals, families, or society. Like most anything, there are pros and cons. I do believe that we must do a better job of understanding the profound role social media has in actively shaping our lives.

When boiled down to 280 characters or less, the complexity and richness of life can easily be misunderstood and lost. Each of our lives is far greater than the sum total of singular tweets, texts, likes, posts, or feeds. Yet we continue to toil away from the comforts of our home, trolling our social networks for a quick attention fix. What are we looking for?

There is comfort in knowing that we are not alone in our thoughts, behaviors, or communities. Social media provides us with connection and a glimpse inside other people's lives. Social media is, like any form of communication, a tool and dimension for exploring and understanding the human condition and relationships. It is not, however, a stand-alone service that embodies everything about a relationship. If used as such, our relationships will surely falter. Social media is not evil, but in the hands of ill-informed and ill-intentioned individuals, it can be a medium and force for proliferating malicious, criminal, unethical, and immoral behavior. The net impact of social media on humanity is only just beginning to be measured and understood. Ten or twenty years from now there likely will be newer technology defined and informed methods of interpersonal and social communication that raise similar ethical and moral debate about their consumption, just as social media has today.

The question we must all continue to ask, no matter what communication mediums we either explore, readily use, or dismiss, is what our intentions and actions have been when using social media and what outcomes and impacts resulted. Social media has brought out a self-centeredness to society. It has magnified the "Me and I" generation. In fact, social media has become thought of as "unsocial." While it provides a platform for everyone to speak, many will still not be heard. It is as if there are a billion people all talking over each other at the same time. "Look at me, see me, hear me, understand me, follow and like me, love ME!"

This discourse plays out publicly and privately as we compete for attention in a world drowning in information and data overload. There is only so much any one of us can absorb, yet we continue to consume and push out data as if we are drug dealers addicted to our own supply. This self-centered behavior has many of us looking like saints as we like every good deed that has ever happened within our networks. But in reality, it is distancing us from true relationships, those that are grounded in the sanctity of friendship, trust, and dignity.

Our multimedia existence has made every one of us marketing gurus and targets. We have become expert at sharing, openly and widely, our point-of-vow (PoV) on anything, but we have not mastered the necessary skill of truly listening to others to empathize with them and increasing our compassion. Social media was designed and intended as a communication medium, but for many, it is a one directional PoV asking the world to provide instantaneous attention, validation, credibility, respect, and honor.

Dignity is born from within us. It lies deep within our hearts, minds, and spirit—our humanity. It is not something that can be outsourced, open-sourced, hacked, or faked. Dignity is the underlying source code that universally connects us without judgment, egoism, or bias. As technology relentlessly shapes our future, more than ever, we need to understand dignity and be prepared to bring this source code forward to inform our products, services, and relationships. Dignity is the glue that will keep us, as individuals and as a society, from becoming unhinged.

Dignity in a Data-Driven World

Like it or not, for better or for worse, we live in a frenzied data-driven world. From before we take our first breath to well after we take our last, streams of data that comprise who we are can be captured, stored, bought, sold, analyzed, and used for public-and-private benefit.

Data represents everything about us, from our prenatal heartbeat to our post-mortem transfer of wealth and everything in-between. Every behavior we have, particularly in our consumer-laden world, produces data. Since the advent of the internet, humanity has been going through a rapid digital transformation. As humans adopt new and exciting technologies and more digital tools, and services, we will become even more reliant on data.

"Digital Transformation" represents our rapid adoption, assimilation, and integration of a broad umbrella of technologies and services including unmanned and autonomous systems, Artificial Intelligence/Machine Learning, Internet of Things (IoT), Augmented Reality (AR)/Virtual Reality (VR), and others, which are converging and pose both opportunity and challenge to humanity.

Data sounds like a relatively inert thing, something that has little meaning or value. It is true, that without appropriate context or purpose, data is relatively meaningless. With the right algorithm, analytical tools, and intent, data can have profound utility and value. Amazon, Alibaba, Facebook, and Google know this all too well. These titans of tech thrive by being "consumer spies" that have mastered the art and science of knowing everything about you! Knowledge is power, and in the tech world, consumer intelligence yields big profits. Not everything is cut-and-dried in applying data science to understand and predict consumer behaviors however. The reason the tech giants make big bucks off you and me is in part that they attract and retain talented individuals who continually seek ways to crack the code on consumer behavior.

The Data-Driven Economy is a "Catch-22"

Consumer-facing tech companies contain massive amounts of computing power and data. As such, they are huge targets for hackers and nefarious actors who attempt, sometimes successfully, to breach the tight security of these firms to steal your personal information. Facebook, which has received an enormous amount of backlash from being hacked during the 2016 US presidential elections following the Cambridge Analytical scandal, admitted that on September 16, 2018, more than 50 million[24] users of their platform were hacked. Recognized as the largest security breach in Facebook's history, it took nearly two weeks for the company to stop this external attack. At the time of the writing of this book, the specific purpose of this significant breach, if there was one, is unknown.

On October 8, 2018, *The Guardian* ran an opinion piece where author Rachel Withers[25] summed up Facebook's misguided conduct and misgivings stating,

> This latest blunder also builds on our picture of Facebook as unreliable and undependable, but this time it's because they can't protect us, not because they won't. The

Cambridge Analytica story was shocking but unsurprising: it revealed that Facebook didn't care about our data, except insofar as it could sell it off, packaging it up for the consumption and use of the highest bidder. While it was scandalous that data-hungry, advertiser-friendly Facebook had even allowed such a feature as the one that allowed people to click away their friends' data, it was in line with their data-hungry, advertiser-friendly MO. The truth about the social network, only vaguely obscured, became clear—Facebook was happy for advertisers to leach our data, to look the other way, as long as it kept advertisers happy—but we kept on using it, taking more personal care. Being on Facebook, for those of us who remained, hasn't felt the same since.

But in this case, it's not just Facebook's callousness and carelessness that's been revealed: it's their incompetence. Facebook missed serious holes in their security system. People didn't (or no longer) expect Facebook to look out for them, but they thought Facebook was smarter than this. The company stood to profit from giving researchers access to our data, but stood to gain nothing from letting hackers access our accounts, other than a PR disaster. While Cambridge Analytica taught us that we can't trust Facebook to take care with our data, this scandal shows that's we can't trust them to take care of our data.

Our data, especially in Facebook profile form, will always be an appealing target to hackers, marketers and cartoonishly evil research firms. This case—so far nameless and perpetrator-less—illustrates that we just can't rely on Facebook to protect it. We can't rely on Facebook's care or their competence to shield us.

—RACHEL WITHERS,
October 8, 2018, *The Guardian*

Rachel Withers' forthright observations regarding the consumer dissolution of trust for tech companies like Facebook are right on point. The challenge and issue is a two-way street.

We cannot ever put down our guard, particularly in this time when personal data is highly sought after, hacking is a daily occurrence, and people's data and digital identities are being manipulated for another person's gain.

In this Catch-22 associated with advancing technology for societal gain, consumers and companies each have a significant role to play. In the case of Facebook and other social media platforms, the past ten years has been a wild, exciting ride of personal and social discovery. I have made this statement before and, it bears repeating: In an era of technology proliferation, ill-informed consumers are just one big real-time market research study with limited control, recourse, or justice.

Consumers, including me, continue to be caught up in the buzz, hype, and excitement of technology and forget what we are actually giving up (or stand to lose) when we sign up and into these digital accounts should our information be breached. Most digital technology companies are built to achieve maximum profitability by scaling their service to reach mass markets. Technology is a high-risk and high-reward opportunity for entrepreneurs. The guinea pig is always the naïve consumer, looking to be either a little out-front, or in-line with the herd. Facebook grew in prominence by socializing a technology that made everyone feel unique, as if his or her voice had a channel to the world. What Facebook has proven, not that it set out to do such, is that relationships are valued first and foremost because of the trust people place in them. In the absence of trust, it does not matter if you have the sexiest technology, car, home, or yacht; if the other party does not trust you, relations are over.

Protecting Your Genetic Code

The Facebook Catch-22 is playing out in other examples of technology proliferation. Take for example the current quandary in front of New Age genetics and genealogy companies including 23andMe and Ancestry DNA. In June 2018 the US Federal Trade Commission (FTC) began investigating how these and other DNA testing companies handle personal information and genetic data of their customers with a specific interest in how it was shared with third parties. In 2018 the pervasiveness and use of third party DNA data became a public-policy question when the notorious "Golden State Killer" was arrested after police in California identified the suspect using publicly available data from GEDMatch, a genealogy research site. Although the accessibility of genetic data in that instance served to capture a criminal, the case opened the door to questions surrounding the moral, ethical, and legal use of data for criminal investigations and other purposes.[26]

DNA data is personal and precious data. It is our genetic code, the blueprint and instructions that make us who we are. In many ways our DNA data is the most sacred data an individual has. However, humanity has not yet treated DNA as privately and securely as it should be. In 2018, for example, a security researcher discovered there was a way to reveal personal account details for more than 92 million customers of MyHeritage, an Israel-based DNA testing service.[27] The researcher was able to unveil personal information including email addresses and passwords. Humans do stupid things all the time.

Right now, millions of humans are giving away their DNA data and information with little understanding or recourse to when, how, where, or in what form that data could be used for or against them. As with many forms of new technology, genetics testing with the power of mining an individual's genealogy provides an intrigue. It is alluring to understand one's past. Who does not want to know where they came from? It is exciting to know what comprises your ancestry. Knowing where and whom you came from tells us so much about the person we are today. However, the appeal of learning you are part North African, Indian, Scandinavian, or Pacific Islander or is coming at an unknown cost and risk.

Personally, I believe humanity should be more concerned about protecting our future than preserving our past. Coupled with advancements in technology that bring the cost of genetics testing down, a good-sized marketing budget, and some fresh, fun, and sexy advertising, DNA companies are gobbling up the blueprint for millions of people who basically want to know more about what makes them unique and are curious about their history. There is nothing inherently wrong with this intent or goal, but one should question the future cost or long-term risk to oneself and current or future family if you participate in this. We learn a great deal from our DNA, and I am definitely not suggesting that ethical companies, doctors, and researchers stop trying to unlock our past to guarantee our future. As a husband and father whose wife and child have serious health ailments and diseases, I know firsthand the power of advancing medicine and technology to enrich people in need of this today.

Data comes in many different forms. The attraction of the data-driven world can be intoxicating. With a click of a mouse followed by a sample of saliva and swipe of a credit card a lot about our past can be revealed. For a reasonable fee, DNA testing companies can provide you with a colorful report of your genetic inheritance and family roots. They don't tell you they also leverage your personal data for their gain by selling information about you to third parties to use for their purposes. Those other purposes, some nefarious and some for the public good, represent the risky scenarios that embody this age of data integrity and dignity. In the case of DNA testing, one has to ask if we will greatly regret in five, ten, or twenty years our giving away our privacy and identity so casually.

The business model for 23andMe and similar companies works well for them, but it is made possible at the expense of our privacy. Trading in on our DNA, only when our goal is to have some interesting but not life-essential information on our family history, does not seem equitable or justifiable given privacy concerns. Think about that. DNA companies appear only to ask a fee and a little saliva to test in exchange for a glossy report informing you of your ancestral roots. There is no guarantee that the DNA testing company can keep your data private and secure from now to eternity even if they claimed that is their intention. Thee risk versus value equation is in the direction of high risk for the consumer and low value for what you get from these companies because of what you are giving away—not just a few hundred bucks—But your amazing DNA code!

There is no doubt that genetics data has a high value to society as well as to individuals. DNA testing companies like 23andMe and Ancestry DNA offer customers consent forms and waivers so that they can bundle elements of your DNA data together with other users to have large data sets of DNA to sell to third parties for use in medical, genealogical, and genetics research. The public benefit of this kind of DNA data accessibility for research cannot be overstated. There are dozens, if not hundreds, of debilitating diseases that can significantly benefit from longer term, larger scale, data-driven epidemiological studies. Multiple sclerosis (MS), cancer, Alzheimer's, Amyotrophic Lateral Sclerosis (ALS), and food allergies are just a few.

Meet George Jetson

Increasingly, every product we encounter has the equivalent of an on-board computer. Today we have "smart" home appliances including refrigerators, clothes washers and dryers, televisions, security alarms, lighting fixtures, trashcans, thermostats, water faucets, vacuum cleaners, and toilets which have been made so with lower-cost electronics and microprocessors. These products serve the same function as their predecessors did, except for the fact that they can now be remotely controlled and monitored with smartphones or through "in-home voice assistants" such as Google Assistant, Amazon's Alexa, and Apple's Siri. Soon perhaps we will do away with the majority of these appliances, as Alice from the Jetsons will be serving our needs within our homes.

"Smart" products deliver, as intended by their design, better functional services, higher quality, greater utility, and improved efficiency. On the back of their "smartness," these intelligent products also generate data. The data enables the safe and efficient operation of the product, as well as supporting the customization of product features to our daily behaviors, preferences, and needs.

An example of this is programming your home's thermostat to align with your family's schedule. In doing so, you can create an indoor temperature that is dialed into your personal preferences. "Smart thermostats" also allow homeowners to manage their home's energy use remotely through their mobile phone. "Smart appliances" like refrigerators can keep track of our grocery list, alerting us when our favorite beverage is running low. Your smartphone smart ovens can be activated while you are running to the grocery store, so that by the time your car pulls into your driveway, the oven is already preheated and at the perfect temperature for you to pop in the fresh turkey and vegetables.

Smart products, powered by advancements in microprocessors (embedded computers), as well as internet connectivity, are putting more power into the hands of consumers to optimize their functionality on our terms, for us to determine when and how we need it. This revolution in smart product connectivity, while exciting and cool, still requires human interaction. The sleek interface of an iPhone, iPad, or any mobile device combined with intuitive software keeps our brains from detecting the fact that we are still at the controls of "things" that we had control over in the first place. While we can remotely control these "smart" products from our designated control panel (mobile device), we still physically load the oven with the turkey, empty the clothes dryer, load the dishwasher, and take out the trash.

Until "Alice" the robot comes into our lives, we likely will not decouple ourselves from the majority of household chores. As technology brings "products to life" we have to be aware if it "sucks the life" out of us. The purpose of technology is to serve some utility, yielding a benefit for the user. This begs the question: Is society effectively served by this, or has it become subservient to our technology of "smart products"? There are benefits and trade-offs to technology, some of which are obvious, others that are less transparent. Society is nearing a time when the self-management of data and information as a byproduct of our "smart product" revolution becomes transparently burdensome. I believe we are at that point in time.

Data and Your Human Rights

The role of your data and the impact on your privacy is at stake as humanity accelerates to connect every device digitally within the Internet of Things (IoT) or Internet of Everything (IoE). Technology purists believe the IoT/IoE can yield a more advanced civilization for humanity by enabling every human to have greater access to education, health care, and other services more efficiently and transparently than ever before. Some believe the IoT and IoE will provide humanity with advancements in autonomy, robotics, energy efficiency, and communications that contribute to a more peaceful and sustainable world.

Sometimes we are aware of the data that we produce, and we have control over it unless our security is violated. Such is the case with our financials (credit card number, checking account, or retirement account numbers), health (DNA, blood type, health history and records, insurance information), household management (utility and phone data and bills, driving and transportation data and bill, or other personal data (driver's license, passport ID, social security number).

But often we are completely unaware that data we produce, which we have limited control over, makes us vulnerable to future data and security breaches (such as use of information in our credit reports or from consumer buying behaviors, social media data/trends, internet data usage, among other habits).

Our life, particularly in the Internet of Everything (IoE) era, is one big data generator. We know that there is not one singular piece of data that embodies our entire existence or which can encapsulate our full life story. Our life is far too complex, inter-connected by trillions and trillions of data points. Increasingly however, computing innovations such as quantum computing (QC), neuromorphic computing (NC), and high-performance computing (HPQ) inclusive of artificial intelligence (AI), machine and deep learning are enabling humanity to collect, codify, and synthesize enormous pools of unrelated data. Will there be a time in the future when human consciousness is digitized so that it can be preserved or even function eternally? What would that kind of technological advancement mean for humanity? There are today, scientists, researchers, ethicists, theologians, mathematicians, engineers, lawyers, and others working on that very question.

Humanity is at a vulnerable inflection point regarding our smart adoption and use of technology. There are "systems-level" issues that technology has a broad impact on, and that humans simply cannot predict. Technology is currently ahead of our collective ability to comprehend what its impact will be on humanity. In a short period we have advanced technologically, primarily to the benefit of humanity.

The rapid ascent of technological prowess has not manifested itself equally around the world. While many people accelerate their use of technology in ways that are beneficial to their life, others fall further behind the technology knowledge-adoption-understanding curve. If this dichotomy of adoption remains, there will be a significant gap between the "haves and have nots." This widens beyond wealth to include access to education, access to economic opportunity, and access to infrastructure that supports protection of human health, the environment, and community development.

Technology and application developers are designing new code and solutions each day. As the advance of digital code butts up against the opportunity to mine the genetic code of human-ity there are sure to be even more significant breakthroughs in medicine and science that will affect human health, performance, and longevity. This is an exciting space for innovation. What's not clear is whether humans have the emotional, spiritual, psychological, and intellectual skills and temperament to absorb the wave of ethical and moral issues that will continue to put our individual and collective dignity in question.

The future is now. In each moment and day that pass, we step deeper and deeper into the muck of a data-driven world. Humanity has collided with the Internet of Everything (IoE), creating our own self-imposed "swamp" that will need to be drained if we are not mindful to what its implications are for humanity. To be clear, advancements in technology and the data-driven economy we now occupy are beacons of hope for humanity. Through better use of the data we have now and the future data we will acquire through advancements in technology, humanity will be able to heal and sustain itself with greater efficiency than ever before. There is great power in this and a very real chance that we will not be able to foresee the moral and ethical dilemmas washing over us, let alone the ways advanced technology can be used against humanity by corrupt actors or simply by the onslaught of technology itself (for instance, by a machine-robot apocalypse).

The human-technology convergence has become an existential question. This is why entrepreneurs Richie Etwaru and Michael DePalma have created a new enterprise, "Hu-manity. co" to address data as a human right. In 2018 Richie Etwaru and Michael DePalma launched "Hu-manity.co" to harness the power of technology so that it can be used for us, not against us in a world where our inherent "human data" is bought and sold in a data marketplace that does not respect our dignity. Hu-manity. co estimates that the "human data marketplace" represents an estimated $150B to $200B annual marketplace.

The company exists to challenge the cold, corrupt, and inhumane transactional data marketplace that sells our data without our consent, authorization, consideration, or compensation.

There are thirty human rights recognized by the United Nations[28] "Universal Declaration of Human Rights." Hu-manity.co wants to make the protection of inherent data the thirty-first human right by allowing consumers to claim our data as our property. As defined by Hu-manity.co, "inherent data[29]" refers to datasets that include our geospatial data, driver and vehicle history, consumer spending habits, medical history, and travel, dining, and recreational habits, as well as our browser and social media data."

In support of this novel objective, Hu-manity.co has created an App, #My31,[30] to enable you to take back control of their data as your personal property, and in the process, recover your dignity. Hu-manity.co created the #My31 App on blockchain technology. The app allows users to declare their data as their property and as "a 31st Human Right." In doing so, users of the app will have a "choice to opt-in or opt-out of the new property-centric marketplace" that encompasses the data-driven world. The efforts of Hu-manity.co are admirable. While it is uncertain how well their app will mobilize and transform the data marketplace, one thing is certain: They represent a next generation of social entrepreneurs and innovators who want to do well by doing good. Grounded in a pure desire to unveil the dark-side of data, Hu-manity.co is motivated to provide consumers with the right tools to take action to have a choice and an empowered voice. By magnifying the indignity that is taking place in the data marketplace, Hu-manity.co has already had a positive impact.

As our data-driven world proliferates, more moral and ethical questions are bound to surface. It is important to be mindful of the wide-ranging ways in which your lifestyle generates data. It is critical to understand, whether we like it or not, or whether we see it or not, that technology and data have become infused within our daily lives. Further, you can have control over the "dignity of your data," including how it is treated (produced, consumed, bought and sold) in the global marketplace.

3

In Search of a Humane Humanity

Humanity is at is best, of course, when it is humane. The current state of global affairs has been shaped heavily by big business, big government, and big media. The growing overt immersion of these institutions into public life has created an "us against them" mentality among citizens and consumers—so much so that public trust in these historically well-respected institutions has dramatically waned in the past five years. As a result, the role of citizens and consumers is rapidly evolving. Empowered by more accessible and real-time data, information, and communications, citizens and consumers now wield greater power at the push of a button to disrupt and transform products, services, industries, and entire institutions. This societal change is embryonic, shifting swiftly and daily as public needs collide and grind against the inertia of inefficient and untrustworthy institutions. The issues are much more entrenched, however.

We are living in an era of mass desensitization where truth in media and society are being called on the carpet right before our eyes. Daily, a wide media coverage of shocking events challenges our values, beliefs, and ethics. School shootings, chemical genocide, child sex trafficking, terrorist attacks, beheadings, natural and man-made disasters, criminal acts of misogyny, racism, and sexual assault drive the 24/7 news cycle. The constant bombardment of violent, grotesque, and outlandish behavior from the media that extends to including tweets, messages, and video images sent to our electronic devices is having an enormously negative impact on the public, particularly an effect on our children. So how do we as individuals, let alone as a community or society, reconcile our values and beliefs with such rapid, persistent, and increasingly atrocious inputs of "real-time and real-world" data and information? Do we really need to see and hear so many of the horrors of daily life to understand the world? I am not suggesting we live in a cave and become numb, dumb, and naïve to what is going on around us or suggesting we turn a blind-eye to those in need.

What I am suggesting is that something is being lost—and perhaps it is our very humanity. Are we losing ourselves amid this constant barrage of negative news or through rapid advancements in technology? Is technology too far ahead of our ability to assimilate it wisely? We are at a critical crossroad of evolution. The paths are very different. One path treats all living things with respect and dignity and can lead us to a truth and understanding of who we are and where we are going—our fundamental morality and purpose. The other path can be a shortcut that views life as a means to an end, a commodity that exists to be manipulated and possibly abused and leveraged and controlled for the gain of a select few. The latter path is the one we are currently on.

Think about some of the stark contradictions that exist throughout the world:

- We can crack the genome; however, we struggle to find ways to solve the problem of drug addiction.

- We can collide particles close to the speed of light to understand the origins of the Universe, but we cannot bring political parties together to address the origins of hatred and violence.

- We fund, fuel, and fly missions to Mars and the outer rings of Saturn, but we struggle to bring the same imagination and leadership to find solutions to eradicate hunger and poverty.

- With technology, we can easily communicate with people half a world away, but often cannot manage to have a neighborly, face-to-face conversation with the people living next door.

I've always been captivated by the contradictions inherent between capitalism and the need for conservation. To grow economically, we "must consume." To protect human health and the environment, we "must curb consumption." It is well established that unfettered unsustainable consumption wreaks havoc on the environment and human health and well-being.

The problem for humanity is not so much that we cannot accomplish what we set our minds to do. If anything, humanity has repeatedly proven itself to be highly resilient, determined, and innovative. During dark times and difficult challenges, we have mustered up the best that we have to give and create a way to survive. Our fate has become more than just about survival. It is about dignity, that is, how we serve each other during our time here on Earth. We are at our most resilient, innovative, and beautiful when we are humane to each other and to all living things. The question then is not about whether we can or cannot accomplish something. It is about our will and sheer determination to decide where to focus our individual and collective energies.

I am no judge or jury of the success of humanity. I'm just an observer who is connecting the paths we have treaded in the past with those that we are choosing for our journey into the future. I am simply asking: Do these options align with your values, morals, and sense of dignity? If not, what role can we serve to scout new paths of enlightenment toward a richer and fuller life for us and our families?

Each of us makes deliberate choices on how we spend our energy, time, and resources. The narrative of our lives has been, for too long, scripted and directed by others. It is time to stop being a bystander of change. Change is inevitable, as is our eventual death. The time has come for all of us, as citizens and consumers, to be in control of our own narrative for creating a beautiful, fulfilling, and consequential life.

If There Is No Place for Hatred, Why Does Hate Persist?

Time may heal old wounds for some. But for most of society the passage of time has yet to prove to be a cure for pervasive hatred. One might assume that in this day and age there is no room for racism, bigotry, sexism, or misogyny. Yet one need to look no further than hurtful words and actions of a US president to recognize that if left uncorrected, expressions of bias, intolerance, and bullying transcend time.

Syracuse University and a "Satirical Sketch"

On April 18, 2018, extremely offensive video surfaced of Syracuse University students who were members of the professional engineering fraternity, Theta Tau. The reprehensible video captured select members of the fraternity speaking and behaving in racist, anti-Semitic, homophobic, sexist ways and being derogatory about people with disabilities. The video showed fraternity members in a ritual-like gathering pledging "to always have hatred in my heart" for African Americans, Hispanics, and Jews.

Ugly racial slurs accompanied their derogatory behavior. It turned out that these were performances by the Theta Tau freshman fraternity pledges who had just become new members. They had quickly thrown together what they thought would be humorous skits making fun of their older fraternity brothers at the night's traditional "roast" in the style of Comedy Central. But somehow things went wildly out of control, and the event intended to be funny and outrageous turned out to be outrageous only in how disgusting it was. The group performing the parody was a diverse mix of people, and some were disparaging their own religion or race by their vile behavior. No one claimed to have been abused by their brothers, and in the video we hear audible protests from members about the behavior and language "going too far."

The nearly six-minute video captures a moment when one fraternity member tells Jews to get in the shower, alluding to the Nazi gas chambers, and includes footage of fraternity members simulating masturbation and oral sex on each other as they use racial slurs and other offensive language.

The release of the video online for everyone to see, including of course the university administrators, set off a flurry of reactions of indignation, rage, and sadness within the Syracuse community. Further compounding the situation was language used by Theta Tau to defend themselves. They dismissed as just a "satirical sketch" their roasting of a fraternity brother parodied as a conservative Republican who is uneducated, racist, homophobic, misogynist, sexist, ableist, and generally intolerant of others.

As soon as University Chancellor Kent Syverud was made aware of the video of the event, he issued a statement:[31]

> Dear Students, Faculty and Staff:
>
> Earlier today, the University learned of extremely troubling and disturbing conduct at one of our professional fraternity chapters, Theta Tau.
>
> Videos showing this offensive behavior have surfaced online. They include words and behaviors that are extremely racist, anti-Semitic, homophobic, sexist, and hostile to people with disabilities. I am appalled and shaken by this and deeply concerned for all members of our community.
>
> The conduct is deeply harmful and contrary to the values and community standards we expect of our students. There is absolutely no place at Syracuse University for behavior or language that degrades any individual or group's race, ethnicity, sexuality, gender identity, disability or religious beliefs.

Upon confirming Theta Tau's involvement, the University's Office of Student Rights and Responsibilities immediately suspended the fraternity, effectively halting all activities. At this time, all evidence has been turned over to the Department of Public Safety, which has launched a formal investigation to identify individuals involved and to take additional legal and disciplinary action.

Syracuse University is committed to fostering a community where all our students feel welcome and are treated with dignity and respect. This behavior is unacceptable and contradicts our moral standards.

What happened at Theta Tau serves as a reminder that violations of codes of honor, behavior, and values will be met with swift and appropriate consequences.

The University will communicate further on this matter later today, including about other steps and resources we will make available to our community.

Sincerely,
Chancellor Kent Syverud

In the hours following the video release, Chancellor Syverud and Syracuse University's leadership took swift action, immediately suspending Theta Tau and ultimately expelling some of its members from the university. Theta Tau delivered a formal statement and apology, but the damage had been done and continued to ripple through the university community. Some of the fraternity members were allowed to return to the university, but many people still felt vehemently impacted by this terrible incident.

The university committed to a full top-to-bottom review of all Greek life policies, activities, and culture. The leadership decided that it would provide mandatory training for all students to address the expectations of student behavior in the culture of the community.

Actions taken included expanding anti-bias training for students and conducting a review by all leadership to examine appropriate training for faculty and staff. Further, the leadership put into place a first-year forum for new students that would deliver a seminar and a forum to address diversity and inclusion, implicit bias, alcohol and drugs, and other topics.

The *Daily Orange*, an independent newspaper run by Syracuse University students called the video "the byproduct of a toxic Greek environment that breeds complicity in exchange for social validation." By April 2018, the Theta Tau fraternity was permanently expelled by the university.[32]

We can try to look at humanity through the limiting lenses of economic, geopolitical, religious, or other ideologies and justify when, how, and why we treat others the way we do. We may stand behind certain decisions on the merits of economic policy, national security, academic freedom, free speech, fairness of college admissions, or some other rationalizing framework. Every decision we filter through these constructs that have inherent bias has an impact on humanity.

Somewhere in this process, the treatment of all humans as equal is disrupted, and sometimes even from the best of intentions, good human beings become marginalized, reduced to a sub-group by irrational people who are wreaking havoc on the rest of the more noble members of our society. This behavior runs rampant throughout society today. Whether it's expressed transparently in a tweet by a sitting president of our country, within the sanctuary and confines of church, or under the veil of secrecy within Greek fraternities, each day the best of humanity comes head to head with people who perpetuate limiting beliefs, irrational thinking, and inhumane behavior.

The unfortunate Theta Tau fraternity event at Syracuse University is indicative of a broader issue within society. Why, at face-value alone, does anyone believe that demeaning and demoralizing others is justified, right, or acceptable in any circumstance? If none of us truly accept hatred in our hearts or within our communities, then why, then, is it playing out daily, right before our eyes, on the news, in our schools and communities? If we denounce hate, then why does hate continue to happen?

PART TWO

★ ★ ★

Rational
Relationships

To live life with a sense of purpose, passion, balance, resolve, and accountability is the beating heart of dignity. It is our responsibility and right to discover where we came from (your past), who we are (your present), and how we will embrace this to attain a better future through a self-directed purposeful existence (your future).

We and our existence together are the common denominators for a more sustainable world. Individually and together, we have the potential and power to enact change and see it through. It takes all of us doing our part, every single day, to attain a better world.

You have likely heard that if there is one constant in the universe, on Earth with living systems, and in life, it is change. Change is always imminent. How we perceive and come to accept this fact is critical to whether we will live a life with dignity or one which cedes to external forces.

The key to changing our relationships with other people and with our living Earth to be more rewarding and fulfilling can begin by our ability to reflect on past relationships, redefine what we expect to attain, and create future possibilities.

4

The Pathway to Rational Relations Begins with Us

I wrote *The Dignity Doctrine* to illustrate how the unproductive divisive culture that has permeated our current local and global affairs is destroying the earth and our well-being. I also wrote *The Dignity Doctrine* to put forth a simple solution whereby we can strengthen our future with a new platform for sustainable living, sustainable business, and sustainable governing. The book and its title, much like my past two books (*The Sustainability Generation* and *Time to Trust*), holds up a mirror to the current state of affairs in the United States and throughout the world. One only need to turn to Twitter or the daily news cycle to see that the world is under constant and extreme fire, figuratively and literally, imposed predominately by ourselves.

Yes, it is we humans, the "most intelligent" of all living species, which has put 7.5 billion people in a precarious place, wedged between the disruptive state of constant change and the calm before a coming storm that threatens global environmental and economic calamity and collapse.

To put it another way, we are just comfortable enough to have the option to watch global despair shakedown on our 4.7 inch, LED-backlit, LCD capacitive touchscreen with 16M colors. We are fully geared-up to entertain ourselves right into Armageddon. Hey, at least we can stay oblivious to our plight until its right at our doorstep and upon us. Right?

Well, my friends, the very fact that an ISIS beheading can be seen by our children on YouTube or that our president can be demeaning to people on a social media platform are enough facts to indicate that the storm is here and is already at our doorstep. It is in our children's bedrooms, classrooms, and our living rooms. It is not enough to say, "turn off or put away the iPhone, iPad, or phone."

We are bombarded at every corner with a new reality show that we are all cast in, whether we like it or not, and whether we get credit or are paid or rewarded for being a part of. It is not the Trump show or the Clinton show. It's not the Kim Jong-un or Putin show. It is not the Oprah show or the Ellen show. It is not "Keeping up with the Kardashians" or the proverbial Joneses. It's also not every social justice awareness, movement, and cause that explodes our Twitter feeds with #MeToo, #TimesUp, #BlackLivesMatter, #DACA, #MuslimBan, #NoBanNoWall, #ClimateChange, #NoBan, #NoWall, #Dreamers, and so on. It's all of these people, causes, and things converging together at once, jockeying for attention and relevance, working together as well as at odds with each other to gain significance, action, and control.

A storm of tweets of 280 characters and memes and hashtags are served up to create mass movements, mass confusion, mass hysteria, and gun tragedies in America and all around the world. The interesting and ironic thing is that amid the highly desensitized culture we've created by consuming and interfacing with mass social media, there are fewer and fewer people going to Sunday "mass" for a time of reflection, forgiveness, rejuvenation, or rejoicing. That is too bad, as we all, including me, could benefit from believing in something greater than the persistent negativity and pandering for our attention that we respond to.

As the one big overstatement and generalization within this book, I'd like to say "We have become a hot mess and need to get our stuff together and our asses in gear." Today we have parents who cannot parent; teachers who cannot teach since they choose not to learn; doctors who know nothing about whole-body health and wellness but everything about pushing lucrative drug-based remedies; politicians who cannot lead a party to a basic decision, let alone a democracy, to attain its highest potential; and business people who get rich from our despair and greed as opposed to our enrichment as a people and society. We the people, my friends, are broken from within. Much of our society is devoid of the inner strength to rise above the noise and confusion and has become desensitized to the realities of our time. We need to rebuild our trust in our community and nation and rebuild ourselves from within to have the strength, courage, and good relationships to allow us to grow.

For example, what is your perception and impression of the world? Is it good or bad? Beautiful or ugly? Full of kindness or hatred? What you see, hear, and experience shapes your perception of truth and helps our understanding and views of other people and the world. Our worldview is always changing. Local, national, and world news and events feed our brains with data, information, images, and stories that shape our knowledge of other people's cultures, religions, and governments.

How much credence should we give the segments of news that are deliberately released and fed to us via cable news, social media, newspapers, digital media outlets, radio, and other sources? That question has been the beating heart of the #FakeNews movement of the past couple years. People around the world have come to recognize and push back on the "big brother, big government, big business" backbone of centralized media which has promulgated over the past forty to fifty years. As "the people" become more discerning about data and information, they have come to question the traditional methods of media delivery.

What was once perceived as an independent and highly trusted industry has become a network focused on entertainment, ratings, political agendas, and commentary. People have discovered that news is only "news" in so far as a highly complex machinery has predetermined that what is being touted as "news" is newsworthy

for their customers. Anything can be news, yet the media industry tends to focus more attention and resources on negative news
than any other content. We do not frequently read or hear many
human interest stories of individual heroism, compassion, love,
empowerment, personal success, and survival even though they
take place every second in our world. Rather, we are fed a diet of
human terror, war, anger, greed, lust, scandal, catastrophe, surrender, and so forth.

It's true that the world is far from perfect and that negative
issues are proliferating each day. To say the media is balanced in
its news reporting would be highly inaccurate. It is not. For if it
were, it would balance it's 30-minute news cycle with "Breaking
News" of amazing stories of dignity, heroism, courage, and empathy. Those stories exist and are told by our media, but they are
few and far between the true attention grabbers that are played
over and over to capture our attention and encourage our fears,
outrage, and hatred. Those lowest forms of human intelligence are
pushed on us as news consumers so that we can remain addicted
to a worldview directed by a media state driven by financial profit,
not the responsibility of delivering balanced news. This is not to
say that there are not independent, loyal, and dignified journalists
and news people in the industry. There are. Just as in any industry (financial services, transportation, agriculture, chemicals, and
biosciences) there are good and bad actors.

The concerning and unwieldy new reality for society is that
it is becoming more challenged and complicated to discern truth
from reality. We are already living in a world of artificial intelligence and augmented virtual reality that we've designed. The
Greek mathematician Archimedes of Syracuse stated, "Give me a
lever long enough and a fulcrum on which to place it, and I shall
move the world." Well, today the lever is a Twitter account and the
fulcrum is a populous that feels as if it has been overlooked and
forgotten by its peers. In the past decade, the foundations of truth,
trust, and justice have been shaken and challenged to their core.

Leaders in government, religion, and industry have been challenged to lead in an era of swift information and social change. Public perception used to be shaped by a man with a microphone. Today, there are billions of microphones and a society that no longer trusts, let alone values, the message coming from one man. As shown in Figure 3 these realities compound our daily routines, we are faced with three fundamental truths:

1. The world is rapidly changing; as it does, it is important to observe and acknowledge the rich diversity of the world.

2. How you choose to engage in what matters at a time of imminent change will dictate your present and future success; recognize the gravity of your existence and understand that you have the ultimate power in accepting responsibility for how you choose to influence and respond to change.

3. The ability to lead change is real; it resides in your ability to build trust, be accountable, and take appropriate action.

The question is, within these truths do we see a future with more clarity or greater confusion? The answer to that question lies within each of us. We can sit idle and continue to be consumers of distorted data and information or we can choose to be engaged citizens that choose to elevate ourselves to our highest purpose and with a common conviction and caring for all humans and all life.

Really, it is that simple. Bad things happen. People are imperfect. Our lives are in a constant change of flux. How we choose to manifest the good within each of us to create and accomplish something great is what makes all the difference. Negativity breeds anger and hatred. Positivity spawns kindness and gratefulness. You can have a profound impact on your life and the lives

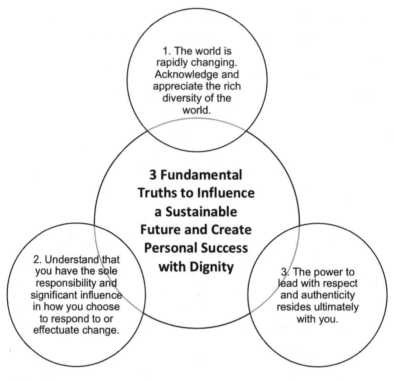

Figure 3

of everyone you meet. It all comes down to mapping out your own doctrine for dignity—that is, how you will deliberately choose to lead a life of purpose, respect, and accountability. Let's get started!

Dignity, the Tie That Binds Us

Regardless of one's situation in life, ultimately we should all be treated as equal. This is not meant to be a political statement or one grounded in a sense of altruism or utopian idealism. As we all know, the unfortunate and sobering reality is that human equality does not exist. In fact, given the state of affairs in the world, one could argue that we are rapidly moving in a direction that devalues human life and dignity and undermines the notion of equality. Name the injustice, and it is happening this very second somewhere in the world: racism, terrorism, prejudice, bigotry, chauvinism, sexism, human trafficking, rape, murder, bullying, misogyny, child abuse, assault, acts of hatred, sex abuse, adultery, crimes of revenge, and so on. Unfortunately, these crimes against humanity are happening everywhere. No one is shielded from the despair and harm that is inflicted from these heinous acts that destroy our dignity.

The one thing humanity has in common as our underlying reality, is a shared space and time, the fact that we are all present and alive in the here and now. We all live under the same stars, sun, and moon. We are all birthed, and someday we will all cease to live in the flesh. No person on this earth is immune to these basic realities of being human. But everyone's life circumstance is different. However, in those differences there are opportunities and hope for making the world a more just, peaceful, and better place, especially during the era we live in for the sake of our children and future generations.

We are all part of one global community of people occupying this planet. For better or for worse, we are a global family. While we are divided by many things—values, geography, economics, political and religious ideology—we are united by space, time, and the beautiful and precious reality we call life. How amazing is it that there are 7.6 billion people in the world—7.6 billion souls that are all seeking love, truth, wisdom, understanding, compassion, and the shear right to live. When life is devalued, when individuals are recognized or treated as less than human and lose their dignity, and when our backs are turned to those in need, ultimately we all suffer.

There is so much happening in the world it is downright overwhelming to keep track of it all. On any given day, there may be headlines of mass shootings, terrorist attacks, foreign espionage, sex scandals, and charges that our government or industries has engaged in illegal acts of greed and corruption. These societal events have been happening for thousands of years.

What is different today, however, is that mass media and technology have converged to magnify these events to such a scale and are bombarded by information about these actions with such frequency and intensity that it is causing us to be overwhelmed, desensitized, and dehumanized. The daily onslaught of images, commentary, audio and video, texts, alerts, sirens, talking heads, headlines, web posts, and tweets has created a hyper-culture of shock and confusion that for many leads to immobility and indifference. Just as I felt immobilized by the cascade of health crises my family faced in a short window of time, when society is constantly assaulted with "Breaking News" of a new, bigger, more glorified disaster, people become hardened and unable to focus attention on creating change by finding solutions to healing and contributing other forces of good.

Negativity breeds more negativity. It is a big giant snowball that brings with it an avalanche of despair. Many humans have big hearts and with this gift a great capacity to heal those who need help, to forgive those that have caused us harm and to love others as we would want to be loved. Today we are all saddled by living in a society where crisis, tension, and entertainment fueled by negativity is the primary common language by which we communicate. This is also the language we are directly and indirectly teaching our kids.

As a diverse group of people bound by space and time, we are first just trying our best to survive, let alone thrive as individuals. However, it is more than possible for every person on this earth to be thriving and living a life of dignity.

How to make it possible for every person on this planet to thrive is not a goal exclusively addressed by economics. It also involves a question of our moral leadership and accountability and having the decency to treat everyone on this earth as we would want to be treated ourselves—with respect, dignity, kindness, and appreciation. All people suffer, if not today, then at some point in our lifetime. Suffering does not need to happen alone; nor does it need to be something that is magnified and made everyone's problem. If we simply recognize that we share a common humanity, that we are all in this together, we can put our shared intellect to the task to solve almost any problem. Together we can rise to accomplish this if we give respect to each person's dignity.

The Dignity Doctrine

• *Dignity begins with you.* There is only one you. Take pride in who you are. Love yourself. Take care of feeding your mind, body, and soul. You are at your best when your personality and energy can shine. Listen to your intuition, and let your gut be your first line of defense and ultimate guide for decision-making. Live life on your terms; after all, it is your life. Give thanks and show gratitude to others and for life in general. Other people, even the nastiest ones, have a heart. In more cases than not, other people are going through a lot of emotional, physical, and spiritual change and upheaval. Be aware and empathetic to others, no matter their disposition. It takes a great deal of diplomacy and effort to be "a better person" or "the best *you*." Very seldom will you be chastised for being truthful, authentic, and compassionate. Being sincere, kind, and unpretentious is an indication of true strength and love.

• *Dignity is an intelligence that resides in all living things.* Value all life and living matter. Respect and celebrate differences and diversity. The world and universe are enormous. We have only scratched the surface of understanding life and its origins. We are part of a complex and interrelated system of matter and intelligence spread across space and time. Earth is a physical boundary, which encapsulates an abundance of life within. We know deep within our souls that we are connected, somehow and in some way, to an intelligence that envelops Earth, yet far supersedes our current ability to comprehend the essence of life. It is that point that lies at the heart of this book. Until we can unequivocally value each other and all life on Earth, we will remain compromised and limited in our ability to attain any understanding of a higher intelligence and certainty beyond our known reality on Earth. We will be too trapped by our beliefs, judgments, and behaviors. Humanity operates at its highest intelligence when it recognizes that all living things are interconnected, part of a shared system, and to be cherished.

  • *Dignity evolves and grows through love of self and life.* Aim to be adventurous, inquisitive, and creative. Your time and that of those you hold most precious to you is too limited not to set your goal to live life to the fullest and enjoy your time with those you love, who are your driving force. Do not allow negative people to push you around, corrupt your soul, or persuade you to do or be anything you do not want. You are the steward of your mind, body, and soul. You are in charge at all times. It is up to you, in every situation, to rise to your greatest self, to be an advocate for you, and to take full ownership over your life and destiny. Over time there will be events, circumstances, relationships, and changes that bring opportunity and challenge into your life. Embrace all of it, every single bit. Each situation will be a chance to learn, grow, and experience life in enriching ways.

Everyone's journey on this earth is different. We all evolve and grow at a rate that is unique to how we choose to experience the world. Do not be too fearful of change or things you do not yet know or understand. Seek out truth, understanding, and clarity. Discover more about yourself by remaining fluid and open to new relationships and what the world has to offer. Close-mindedness leads to isolation, fear, paranoia, hatred, and despair. Remain resolute in your core convictions but responsive to change and matters that are out of your control. Everything around you can be in flux, but ultimately you can remain levelheaded, aware, and ready for action.

"You, Me, and We" Are the Future: The Sustainability Generation

It has been eight years since the publication of my first book, *The Sustainability Generation: The Politics of Change and Why Personal Accountability is Essential NOW!*. The *Sustainability Generation* demonstrated how a new and enlightened generation of political-government-business-community leaders, educators, innovators, and practitioners has evolved to contribute to a more peaceful, just, and sustainable world. I put great emphasis on the impact of our consumptive lifestyles and the role each of us play as citizens and consumers toward attaining a better world today and for our children.

Eight years is not a very long time; however, a great deal of change has occurred between 2012 and 2020. One observation that I am happy to report is that "sustainability" is now widely discussed as a framework for governments, corporations, individuals, and other institutions. A mainstreaming of sustainability continues to unfold as major global corporations, including leading-edge technology companies and religious institutions, including the Catholic Church, as well as city and county governments, the military, and many other institutions continue to adopt principles of sustainability into their culture and policies.

It is well known that a one-size-fits-all approach to sustainability does not exist, nor would we want it to. Sustainability is about discovering and embracing how you (your family, community, organization) define your goals of having sustainability.

To be attainable and have an impact, sustainability should be customized to the context of your life—to your needs, goals, and purposes and also in the context of the resources and other situational factors available in your environment. The reality is that there will be trade-offs and alternatives, but the likelihood is that achieving sustainability depends on using the following principles:

Restraint (using resources less with more efficiency or even optimally)

Compromise (to reach mutual and equitable allocation of resources so everyone has an opportunity to meet their basic needs)

Collaborative creativity (working constructively with others to find innovative solutions to these challenges and to our well-being)

Global awareness of sustainability has increased in the past decade. I'm using the word "sustainability" liberally here to refer to a broad scope of opportunities, agendas, innovations, and initiatives for survival in the face of natural and human-induced changes that threaten the attainment of the basic needs of humanity—food, clothing, shelter, connection to others, and respect and love. In retrospect, it makes sense that the goal of sustainability has taken on greater meaning and purpose in society. As the world becomes hotter, more "global," and more crowded, we are challenged to do more with less and reconcile our individual wants with the needs of a worldwide society. In the near future (the next two decades), the interrelated challenges facing humanity today are likely to magnify and quite possibly erupt like hot magma bursting from the Kilauea Volcano, sending billions of people in retreat and a search for safety, security, and the ability to sustain themselves. We need a unified humanity to step up to the challenge of preventing explosive problems in the next ten-to-twenty years. This includes the dangers of the following:

- More frequent and severe economic swings in global financial markets, currencies, stock market returns, and other financial fundamentals that swiftly impact the wealth of nations, corporations, and individuals

- Increased security breaches of personal information exposing billions of people to identity theft, as well as severe cybersecurity attacks of organizations that pose a significant risk to public-and-private infrastructure and threaten human life, health, and the environment

- An increase of social inequity and economic and social injustices resulting from racism and bigotry combined with the government's economic problems over funding social security, health care, affordable housing, and programs that provide safety-networks to prevent social dysfunction, mental illness, suicide, and mass shootings

- A deepening of political divides based on social instability, particularly in developed nations

- Supply-chain and market-price instability affecting the availability and price of commodities such as oil and gas, precious metals, and agriculture products like sugar and coffee

- Increase in the intensity and severity of climate impacts including severe weather and natural disasters, particularly in highly populated urban and coastal regions

- Mass migrations of people from war-torn regions that face continued geo-political and religious conflicts

- Natural resource constraints and conflicts, particularly over the equitable allocation of clean water and safe and nutritious foods

- An escalating intolerance, particularly among younger generations, for inept leadership that doesn't acknowledge or address the realities of climate change and

associated social and economic inequities or deliver
of more progressive policies and solutions

If humanity continues down the same path of behavior which got us to 2020, it is reasonable to assume these urgent problems may very well mark our reality over the next two decades. However, if we take stock of these realities and choose to modify our behaviors, humanity can change course and rewrite its future. The current state of affairs in the world is not something that is simply happening to us. It is the future that was defined by us and our predecessors by virtue of our past relationships and actions.

The future is not something we step into; instead it is something defined by how we live right now. Therefore, if we want to change the trajectory of humanity we have to change how we see ourselves and how we interface with each other in this very moment. If we see each other as adversary and foe, we will shape our future accordingly. If we view each other with respect and have a sense of mutual obligation for attaining a better future together—well then, we will do just that.

Much time and effort is spent on forecasting and predicting the future. What will tomorrow bring? What will my life be like in five or ten years? Whom will I marry? Will I have kids? Will I lose my hair by age 50? Will we occupy the moon or Mars by 2050? Too often we put too much credence on what will happen in the future. Many have heard the phrase "The future is now." The future IS now, right here in this moment, as you read the words on this page. We shape the future with our actions in the moment. If our actions are productive and positive, our future has a better chance of yielding similar outcomes. If our actions are unproductive and negative, our future will likely be impacted accordingly. We all have the aptitude to shape our own futures. We accomplish this through mindful deliberation and decision-making.

While sustainability is often couched as a philosophy for reconciling the impact we have on future generations, in practice, sustainability is actually about having an impact here and now in the moment. That can be material (meaning focused on resource utilization, waste and efficiency and restoration of environmental damages), or it can be non-material impact that is equally important (i.e., intellectual, spiritual, cultural). Non-material impacts often influence short- and long-term material impacts. Humanity's moment is not some place off in the distant future. We cannot sit idly by and hope for a better future to evolve at the whim of politicians or the magic of innovators. Humanity's moment is right now—right within the grasp of our hands, hearts, and minds. The question is, what are you doing about shaping your future for the better, right now?

I hope that in reading this book, there will be nuggets of wisdom that spawn ideas and actions for you to embark on to create a blueprint for your better future. Do not wait another second to do this. In fact, you can grab a pen and paper and write down answers to the following questions:

> What is most important to my life and me?
>
> What do I believe in?
>
> Who am I right now, today, in this moment?
>
> Whom do I wish to become, starting right now?
>
> Why am I here?

We may not know the answer to last question. Few do. The answer can and will reveal itself with enough patience and perseverance. You can decide to think about the questions and come back to them every few days, or weeks, and definitely ask this of yourself each year. Do you then have a good idea of your life's purpose?

If you are not one of the 40 million people who bought a copy of Rick Warren's book, *"The Purpose Driven Life,"* let me kindly recommend that as a resource to explore. Originally published in

2002, the book has become a global movement, focusing people on how to simplify and enrich their lives through daily inspiration and a more focused mindset on living in the now with greater personal fulfillment, satisfaction, and meaning. I have read the book and use it often as a guide when I am feeling a bit overrun by life's demands. By the way, "life's demands" are only demands insofar that we make them so or allow them to be. Once we understand that we are the stewards of our time, energy, and capacity to give and receive love, we are one step closer to living a more enriched and amazing life.

My wife and I now have two boys, now ages nine and eleven. Over the past eight years, our boys have grown with the curiosity and wonder that seems to be found only in children. Their innocence and interest in the world is still relatively pure, leaving them unbiased and open to exploration, self-discovery, and new ideas. As a parent, I feel that I have come full circle in my life. I continue to believe that a pathway to influence politics, business, innovation, technology, and "the world" as a change-maker and "leader" is to jump in and take swift and persistent action. However, I have also come to understand and appreciate that we must invest more in our children. Our children represent the next generation of change-makers, innovators, and doers. They are growing up in an era of significant distrust, tremendous change, great technological advancement, and much political posturing and civil unrest. Each successive generation has a carryover of compounding social, economic, and environmental challenges.

In 2019 Amnesty International published findings of their *"Future of Humanity"* survey at the UN Climate Change Conference to mark Human Rights Day. Amnesty International surveyed over 10,000 Generation Z (18–25-year-olds) across 22 countries, asking them about the most important issues facing the world and facing their country. The survey also asked Generation Z about who they felt was responsible for addressing the challenges. The *Future of Humanity* survey revealed the following:

- Climate change was the most frequently cited by Generation Z respondents (44%) as the most important issue facing the world.

- Second to climate change was pollution (36%) and terrorism (31%). At a national level, Generation Z respondents highlighted corruption (36%), economic stability (26%), pollution (26%), income inequality (25%), climate change (22%) and violence against women (21%) as the most pressing concerns facing their country.

- When asked what is needed to address these pressing challenges, the majority of Generation Z respondents (73%) said that protection of human rights was essential, even if it had a negative impact on the health of the overall economy.

Further, the Amnesty International survey revealed that 73% of Generation Z (Gen Z) respondents said "governments should take most responsibility for ensuring human rights are upheld-rather than individuals (15%), businesses (6%) and charities (4%).[33]

While independent surveys of different age groups like millennials (Gen Y) and Gen Z will reveal different attitudes and opinions of the world around us, there are some things we also agree upon. A 2019 survey conducted by ypulse.com of Gen Z and millennials' views on the United States found that 86% of 13–17-year-olds and 79% of 18–36-year-olds are "worried" about the future of America. More specifically, the majority of both generational groups said they believe "that the world is a chaotic place right now" and that "something catastrophic will happen in the next 5 years." Climate change ranked #1 as a top issue of concern in the ypulse.com survey of Gen Z and millennials.[34]

An important distinction found between Gen Z and millennials in the ypulse.com survey was that Gen Z ranked "social media" and "technology addiction" as their next two top issues, whereas millennials ranked "debt" and the "economy" as their next two top concerns. While the generational insight from these surveys is interesting, what's important to understand is that fear, anxiety, and a feeling of uncertainty and dread permeate the perceptions of how our youth think about the current state of our county and the near-term outlook for the United States and the world. Gen Z and millennials have become disillusioned and lack foundational trust in what were once considered traditional pillars of society in business, government, education institutions, the media, and nongovernmental organizations. Our youth represent what Deloitte calls a "generation disrupted." While some view them as pessimistic, Gen Z and millennials are seeking greater transparency from their leaders and calling for swifter intentional actions to address the social, economic, and environmental concerns they have.[35]

The best way to mitigate the crippling uncertainty of the generation's angst is to work together with them to take action on improving the state of the world We must devote our attention to their education, wellness, and development. Our children are the Sustainability Generation, those that will assume responsibility for their lives and this earth we all occupy. As they do this, will they have the courage, commitment, creativity, and collective consciousness to cultivate dignity and respect among all living things? Or will many grow into an existence marked by unconscious patterns and behaviors of indifference? Our children and youth represent a hope and promise for creating a better world. They are a rejuvenation of life, capable of shaping their lives to be enriched by peace, dignity, and love. The greatest opportunity humanity has to create a more just and sustainable world resides not in the policies or processes we design and enact but in how we act as adults.

Our mindset, consciousness, philosophy, and behavior are reflected in how our children behave and the kind of persons they are. What we do, how we act, and who we become all have an effect on our children. To influence change you must be (and live) the change. If we want to see the next generation thrive, we must show them through our own behaviors and teach them the best of our collective intellect and wisdom so they have a more solid foundation to build on and make positive change. In shaping the future of our children's lives we ultimately shape the fate of humanity.

We do not need (necessarily) a revolutionary change in technology or a new product, service, gadget, or App to download to "save" the world. What we need is a reality check, perhaps a swift kick in the ass, to get everyone doing their part to assume responsibility for our way of life and the lives of those around us. Happiness, acceptance, peace, love, and sustainability—do not need to cost a lot. What they do require, however, is that we respect one another, live each day with a sense of purpose, and discover that we can accomplish great things when we work together.

In the past, I have often described sustainability as a journey, which I believe it is. The goal of sustainability is both a personal and collective journey. It is also much more than a journey; it is a right. And it is the responsibility, obligation, and conviction that any human must have every opportunity to not only survive but to live life and thrive. The journey and road to arrive at this will be different for everyone. Together we can ensure that the fundamental right to live, and opportunity to be loved, is attainable by everyone.

I am reminded by a now famous quote Hillary Clinton used during the 2016 election campaign. Often attributed to Harriet Tubman, this has never been proven to have originated from the great American abolitionist who once resided in Auburn, New York, my hometown. Clinton's 2017 book *"What Happened"* contains these well-known words:

If you are tired, keep going.
If you are scared, keep going.
If you are hungry, keep going.
If you want to taste freedom, keep going.

This quotation should hold great meaning and significance for anyone who admires the incredible courage and strength of Harriet Tubman who escaped to freedom and then contributed so much as a conductor on the Underground Railroad to helping others find freedom. It is an inspiration to those of us who are average people who hopefully have nothing like the terrible obstacles she faced, but who work hard every day and struggle with difficult situations to make a better life for ourselves and our family. This is a powerful reminder that we all must chart and stay a course. Many, if not most of us, will encounter significant challenges in our lives. Our temperament, faith, and values will be tested. Our skills and strength will be pushed to their limits. Our frustration will show and our fears will be revealed. But hopefully we keep going.

When "Disorder" Is a Gift: The By Kids For Kids Story

I first spoke with Norm Goldstein in 2017. A colleague had made me aware of an innovative organization serving youth called By Kids For Kids (BKFK, bkfkeducation.com) and suggested I research them. When I read about their co-Founder, Norm Goldstein's incredible background and family story, I was certain I wanted to reach out to him and request a time to talk.

Norm Goldstein and his family are the definition of resilience, creativity, and ingenuity in the face of personal challenge. Like many entrepreneurs, Norm Goldstein has a panache for storytelling and action. When we spoke on a fall afternoon in 2017 he told me about his youth and how he was a passionate boy, interested in a lot of things, and found it challenging to focus his mind in school and at home. He said that he was an "inquisitive child" who found himself having all kinds of issues at school, home and in the community. He realized that he "could not be contained within structured environments."

Norm told me that it was tough going for a while since his parents didn't understand why he behaved more erratically than others, let alone really understood him. Over the years Norm discovered that his being unsettled was also a strength, particularly since he saw himself "always problem-solving beyond the obvious solutions." This gift led Norm down the path of entrepreneurship since he felt most comfortable thinking outside the box, seeing opportunity in things "hidden in plain sight." Norm learned to harness what most people saw in him as a shortcoming into a passion for discovering solutions and creating business enterprises from "obvious needs."

Norm went on to tell me more about his family. He said it wasn't until he had kids of his own and discovered they exhibited many similar learning and development traits at an early age that he began to understand attention-deficit/hyperactivity disorder (ADHD) as being linked to genetics and heredity. Norm talked about his three children, two of whom have ADHD, and one in particular, his daughter Cassidy, who was fortunate to benefit from having a sibling that preceded her. When she was 11 years old, Cassidy began to receive tutoring for her needs.

Norm explained that a tutor had been assigned to Cassidy asked her to complete a drawing assignment. The tutor wanted to observe how she interpreted her backyard landscape and provided Cassidy with crayons and paper to draw a picture of her backyard. Norm said that Cassidy would break crayons into smaller pieces, partly because of the pressure she put on writing objects and also in an attempt to manage her dexterity so that she could more accurately draw the picture she had in mind.

The broken crayons were small and hard for Cassidy to maneuver. The first assignment proved to be challenging. The tutor asked Cassidy to continue to work on the assignment and that he would return within a week. When the tutor visited Cassidy a week later, to his and her father's and her father's great surprise, she revealed a beautiful interpretation of her backyard, wonderfully drawn and colored. The tutor asked Cassidy how she was able to control her hands to draw such a beautiful picture. She said, "with these!"

Cassidy presented them with twelve crayons that had been inserted into a plastic tubes. The tubes served to elongate the crayon and enabled Cassidy to put the right amount of pressure on the broken crayon stubs in a manner that stabilized her hand and ability to control her finer motor skills. The result was astounding, allowing Cassidy to translate the image of her backyard within her brain to a splendid interpretation in her drawing.

Cassidy was asked by the tutor and her father how she had thought of such a good solution for her use of drawing tools. The day prior Norm had purchased a dozen roses for his wife. The roses came with a tube around each stem to hold them upright in the bouquet. After his wife put the roses in a vase she discarded the tubes. Cassidy had seen the tubes in the trash and thought that a crayon might fit perfectly inside the diameter of the tube. So she tested her hypothesis only to discover she had invented a wonderful aid to illustrating.

Norm and the tutor were speechless. Norm, who knew a good idea when he saw it, had a colleague conduct a patent search to determine if there was prior devices registered for this type of drawing aid. It was determined that there were about 20 existing similar patents for the holding of objects. Cassidy became very engaged in working hard with her father to make a unique product and write their patent claims. The effort took over three years of research and refinement. At the age of 14 Cassidy became one of the youngest in the country to be issued a patent by the US Patent and Trademark Office for her invention. Norm and his daughter went on to license the invention which was ultimately sold through Walmart.

Norm and Cassidy's incredible journey did not conclude with the launch of a product. Their experience created a movement, where kids could become the beating heart of invention and innovation. In 2003 Norm and Cassidy cofounded their "pro-social" company called "By Kids For Kids" (BKFK). Together the father and daughter team began inspiring educators around the country to teach how the process of creative problem solving and critical thinking could be structured into curriculum for students. They engaged a cohort of 20 education experts and launched with support from Xerox a curriculum that aligned with national standards. BKFK also partnered with Scholastic, the National Education Association (NEA), and other Fortune 500 companies to roll out their "Inventive Thinking Toolkit" for educators focusing on school districts with underserved youth in key areas across the United States.

Because of the tremendous reach and success of BKFK, the innovative kid-based entrepreneurial education program focused on Norm's method to "create-innovate-manage-build" began to have a significant social impact and garner more visibility. It wasn't too long before it caught the attention of Berkshire Hathaway's Chairman and CEO, the financial icon, Warren Buffett. A long supporter of education and youth, Warren Buffett decided to work with BKFK to create a unique opportunity to launch a new high-impact financial literacy program.

Today, BKFK's *Warren Buffett's Secret Millionaires Club* Learn and Earn program and animated TV cartoon series teaches financial literacy and entrepreneurship through family-oriented home-based and classroom activities for students. The program is run as a competition across different age groups and grades. Each year a handful of team finalists are flown to Omaha, Nebraska to present their business ideas to Warren Buffett and a panel of distinguished judges. Finalists and the winning ideas are awarded prize money, and in some years receive shares of Berkshire Hathaway B Stock.[36]

Since its inception, BKFK has specialized in "creating dynamic educational programs designed to develop 21st century skills." BKFK provides and delivers free, customized "innovation-powered" educational initiatives for schools, families, and others based on current educational standards. BKFK programs have been purposefully designed to engage and stimulate kids critical and creative thinking skills and support healthy living, financial literacy, digital citizenship, and standards-based content and enrichment for science, technology, engineering, art and math (STEAM). Since its launch in 2003, BKFK has partnered with many incredible organizations including Disney, Sikorsky Aircraft, NYSE, NBA, NFL, Intel Foundation, MLS, National PTA, Sallie Mae, Junior Achievement, Girls Inc., and 4H.[37]

After nearly fifteen years of operation, Norm has had the privilege of working successfully to deliver innovative programs in partnership with public-and-private partners from public school districts, global corporations, leading-edge socially-focused foundations, not-for-profit organizations, and true leaders like Warren Buffett. I asked Norm about where he saw the future of education in America.

The consummate entrepreneur who is continually improving and shaping the future, Norm spoke about the need to "create unique platforms to address the changing educational environment." He said there will be specifically a need to quickly investigate how best to elevate technologies such as Virtual Reality (VR), Augmented Reality (AR), Artificial Intelligence (AI) as ways to engage, educate, and inspire the next generation of students.

Norm stated that there is a bubbling up of technology that is creating disruption across multiple industries and services. These technologies are rapidly shaping our future, a future which will require each of us to transform how we learn, live, work, and play. Norm sees traditional education delivery and models as rapidly becoming outdated and needing to be augmented with new technology if they are to stand a chance of not being fully disrupted.

Norm added, "ADHD runs in my family; it's genetic. What was once a disability has turned into an asset. We need to start seeing the obvious opportunities right before our eyes. Much like Cassidy linked discarded plastic tubs with broken crayons, our opportunity now is to solve social needs without limitation or constraint."

Truly, the need for change in America's education system is greater than ever. Technology provides an opportunity to enliven inspiration and innovation within every child. If augmented properly, technology can be an enabling force to ensure ever child is lit up and excited about learning and shaping their future, particularly children with special needs who are often underserved or lost in the cracks of inefficient and dated education delivery models.

Much like Norm and Cassidy who rose above the stigma and realities of ADHD and other challenges, we must resolve to look deeper at our inherent biases and not see ourselves or other individuals as trapped by our deficits, but as people with the potential to be shining beacons of hope and opportunity. Norm and Cassidy's heartwarming and inspirational story reminds us that no matter what life may throw at us, we can as Norm told me "always find a way to turn lemons into lemonade."

5

Reflecting on the Past, Emboldened by the Future

Something happened to me when I hit 40. It was not a mid-life crisis, but it was an awakening of sorts. The contrast was not subtle. As if a switch had been turned on, I began to see life much differently. Things that used to matter to me faded away as other priorities and stimuli competed for my attention. Certainly, the medical and emotional challenges my wife, son, and family experienced in a short duration of time had a profound impact on all of us.

It was as if one day I woke up and realized I had been changed. My brain was rewired. For a long time I had felt the desire to grow further, to build and pursue the future that could bring me joy, happiness, wealth, recognition, and love. For some reason I began to feel a sense of freedom from a constant growling and inner conflict between my id, ego, and superego. This was logical, as for a number of years I bore witness to a sequence of life-changing events with my wife and son that my mind tried to rationalize and comprehend and which challenged me to grow, personally, intellectually, and spiritually.

I cannot say there is anything that profound about my following conclusions, but for some reason they hit me like a ton a bricks shortly after I turned 40.

- There are no rules about pursuing the best lifestyle (except about staying "within the law," of course!).

Define and live by the rules that work for you. Do not live your life for anybody else.

- Get out of our head. Too often, our overly critical "thinking brain" rules our mindset and behavior. Our brains are hardwired for survival. Taking risks are not intuitive for most people. Resultantly, we can be our own worst enemy when it comes to personal growth, happiness, and fulfillment. The freedom to flourish in life is as much a result of an emotional, spiritual, and psychological mindset as it is a result of environmental or material advantages that encourage manifestation of our human potential.

- Power and leadership are subjective. Most people try to attain them throughout their careers and in the titles they work hard to achieve and identify with. Those that have it often abuse it. The reality is that power and leadership are traits everyone can manifest and wield. True power and leadership is underserved, underappreciated, and under-taught. You do not need a formal title to live a life with purpose and to be a leader. You just need to be yourself and allow your intellect, passion, and energy shine through in all that you do.

- I owe it to myself and you owe it to yourself and your immediate family to be your best self.

- We should "follow the money." Having money does not equate to personal wealth, happiness, or security. But you should not fear or loath a healthy pursuit of money. If you are like millions of others who find yourself "financially stressed," follow the money to get to the root cause of your unhappiness. What you may find is that money is not necessarily the problem. Rather, something altogether different is what distresses you.

- We shouldn't "sweat the small stuff." Life is full of up's and downs. What you think is a big deal today will likely look miniscule ten years from now.

- We should take care of our mind, body, and soul. Exercise, eat healthily, drink more water, turn off all electronics and go for a walk. Read a book or do absolutely nothing but feel the breeze on your skin.

- Egotism, unfortunately, often supersedes spirituality and selfless service to others. We exist in an ego-driven world. Be mindful of how much your ego drives your behaviors, relationships, and happiness. Take the time to redefine (if it is lacking) what spirituality means to you and how it can be enveloped into your life. Also, think about your life's purpose. We are all here for a purpose. Work to understand what motivates you, what makes you feel energized and alive. How can you bring your best self to every situation? Leading a better, more dignified life begins and ends with your ability to live up to your fullest potential. It is in our service to others where we begin to create meaning and understand why we are here.

- Death is a natural and spiritual part of everyone's lifecycle. Our comprehension of life is limited to the physical form of our bodies. We fear death largely because we do not know what, if anything, is beyond the certainty we have when living in the here and now. To fear death is futile and diminishes our capacity to live and love today. The sooner we accept this reality, the sooner one can begin truly feeling alive and living an incredible life.

- We should make the effort to show more kindness, gratitude, and eagerness—and try smiling more! First and foremost, the world wants to see our smile. Secondly, it wants to know that we are open to what it has to offer us, so when we are kind to others, they in turn will be kind to us. Demonstrating eagerness for life and for relationships and showing gratitude for others' time, energy, and resources is what lifts us.

- Let your spirit and energy shine through. There is only one *you*. If your light is beautiful, let it shine through in all its whimsical, humorous, fun-loving grandeur and glory. Do not let other put you down or temper your personality to fit their view of who you should be or how you should act. You are at your best when you are allowed be your best. Respect this privilege, and more importantly, never let others disrespect you if you feel you deserve respect.

People long for identity, belonging, influence, certainty, and self-preservation. Each of these reveal and validate the human ego for survival. We do not spend enough time, in general, working to serve humans at the front-and-back-end of life (birth and death). Our greatest efforts are selfishly spent on how we want to be perceived, liked, and loved rather than how we should love others.

My Personal Reflection on Fear and Courage: In the Abyss of the Unknown, Life Is What You Choose to Make of It

I feel guarded when sharing personal information and "my story." I am mindful that there are millions if not billions of people in the world who get up every single day with one goal—survival. Often they face their personal challenges in spite of real despair over their economic, environmental, and social conditions. However, when I think about what my wife and sons went through in a short period, I know that we, like billions of others, have faced "the abyss of the unknown," those challenges that get thrown at you in life, which leave you feeling targeted and feel insurmountable to overcome.

This is not a story about turning the lemons that life throws at you into lemonade. We all know we can put a positive spin on life's difficulties. This is a story of self-respect and courage in hard times and rejoicing and rejuvenation that we made it through. It is about realizing that even in our darkest of hours we can cultivate and elevate a spirit of hope and humanity to become higher versions of ourselves, and as a result, better the lives of the people and the world around us.

To start, let me say I did not even realize how much my family and I were suffering. Over a relatively short period, so much had occurred in our lives that jumping from crisis to crisis began to feel normal. It was nearly impossible to process all that was happening in the moment. To provide some information about our grave situation, I'd like to first lay out some facts. Over the course of five years, the following sequence of events transpired in my family:

March 2008 – Our first son Owen is born, exactly on his due date, by emergency caesarian. The day began with a banter with a doctor-in-residence who said with a matter of fact tone, "Ya know, just because it's your due date, that doesn't mean you had to come to the hospital!" Both my wife and I looked at the woman with what must have been perplexed yet demonic eyes. Did she really think we drove ourselves up to the hospital and into the emergency area because this was on our to-do list? Perhaps my wife did not look like Linda Blair in *The Exorcist*, but she was clearly in labor. The doctor-in-residence continued to treat us like a couple of imbeciles who arrived at the hospital because we simply had it on our calendar. Well, to be honest, we did have the date circled on the calendar, but rest assured, we were there because my wife

Aileen was in real labor. The doctor-in-residence's reaction always stuck in my mind, as it was a precursor, a foreshadowing perhaps, of a sequence of events, some that were fortuitous, others that were as cold and crass as the doctor-in-training was.

My wife had been in labor for a full day and was about eight centimeters dilated. The doctors kept waiting for the baby to descend further. After hours in labor, the baby's heart rate began to escalate, as did my wife's heart. The doctors made the decision to take invasive action. Just before 9:00 p.m. our son Owen was born. He was as red as lobster, but he and the room were silent. Aileen told me later that she was waiting to hear the wail of his presence. But the nurses shepherded him away immediately. He spent four days in the intensive care unit (ICU) for having a blockage near his lung and some breathing difficulties. The blockage dissipated and Owen is released to mom after four days. He has a difficult time breastfeeding, there is little support for my wife to nurse, and staff tells us to use bottles to get him feeding before they will release him and his mom from the hospital.

2009 – The first year to eighteen months of Owen's life were overwhelming. He was a beautiful baby, but also very colicky. My wife and I had heard from others about colic, but we were so consumed with Owen's needs we never realized we were in the midst of parenting a colicky child because we discovered Owen had a perfect storm of autoimmune diseases including severe food allergies, asthma, eczema, and eosinophilic esophagitis (EE).

The spring of 2009 – About a year after Owen's birth, Aileen had a miscarriage. It was a crushing experience. She was eight weeks pregnant when it occurred. The pregnancy was something we both wanted, and it brought us a great deal of happiness to learn that she was pregnant again. The loss of the baby was very hard for both of us, but particularly for Aileen. She had been going through a lot, feeling secluded in our home in Rochester, New

York, finishing her master's degree and caring for a colicky baby for the past year. She was also in the middle of finishing her master's degree. The pregnancy seemed to elevate her spirits. When the miscarriage occurred, it was devastating. Later that year however we would again be pregnant and spent every second of a 9-month journey relishing in the experience.

2010 – Our second son, Neal is born, also by caesarian, but it was not an emergency. Aileen's water broke early in the morning. She was thrilled because she was bound and determined to have a vaginal birth. After taking months of prenatal yoga, she felt ready. Although she knew she had prepared for a natural birthing experience, she changed her mind at the last moment and said she'd rather have the repeat cesarean because she didn't want to start the process and experience an emergency again. The birthing experience was completely different than Owen's. Neal was born under a much calmer situation. Given what Aileen and I experienced in Owen's birth, I was guarded and nervous about Neal, but his birth went very well. He immediately nestled with mom and began breastfeeding. Neal's birth was triumphant. That beautiful day was also marked by confusion and concern.

I remember vividly the moment just after Neal was born when the doctor called a nurse over to him. The doctor was working to put Aileen back together again, so to speak. The doctor then called over another doctor and nurse. There were three people standing over her looking at the incision area where Neal had just emerged. The surgical area was covered from my view as I sat on a stool next to Aileen holding her hand through the procedure. She squeezed my hand and quite frequently looked into my eyes for a sense of certainty that it was all going okay.

Aileen was highly apprehensive about Neal's birth, particularly after the experience she had with Owen. She asked if everything was all right. Neal was crying in the background. Tears of joy streamed from my wife's eyes as she heard the baby. I told her everything was great. I was caught between the joy of seeing and hearing Neal for the first time and reassuring Aileen about the birthing process, and the distraction of the doctors who appeared to be perplexed by something.

All I remember is a doctor handing something to a nurse and asked it to immediately be sent for analysis. The doctor then his completed his work to stitch up Aileen, and mom and our newborn baby were taken to a recovery room.

I went to the waiting room area to let some family members know about the successful birth. When I made my way to Aileen's room, her mom was there, and Aileen was with the baby. She seemed a little concerned. She let me know that the doctors had removed a tumor from her ovaries and had sent it out for a biopsy to determine whether it was benign or malignant. I remember her aura clearly; Aileen looked very peaceful as she held Neal. Her mom on the other hand seemed very nervous and unsettled. The nurse said it would be some time, perhaps a few hours or a day or so, before the results from the biopsy would be received.

Within hours, and on the back of a magnificent and beautiful birth, we learned that the tumor was malignant. It seemed like the sobering reality that Aileen had cancer did not have time to sink into our minds. All that we knew was that Aileen would require more testing and consultation to determine what kind of cancer it was, whether it was contained or had spread, and what the next steps would be.

Despite our anxiety, much of the next few months were happily spent taking care of two boys; a courageous and adventurous two-year-old and an adorable newborn baby with bright blue eyes. During this time, it was determined that Aileen had ovarian cancer. Several treatment options were presented to Aileen. Her doctor suggested that ultimately removing the uterus and ovaries would limit her long-term risk of the cancer spreading. The survival rate for woman with ovarian cancer is high if the cancer is found at an early stage.

Aileen often reflects about the birth of Neal and the revelation that her cancer was in an early stage. When she was about to give birth to Neal she had the option to have the caesarean or to have a vaginal birth. She chose the caesarean because she had one with Owen and felt this procedure would be best for Neal. As it turns out, that decision saved Aileen's life.

Aileen ultimately made a very difficult personal decision and chose to have a full hysterectomy. Her logic was that this was the best choice to having the opportunity to live as long a life as possible with her family. She felt blessed to be a mother of two boys, and since the birth of Neal exposed her cancer, it was a sign that she should not take the risk of waiting to have surgery. She could then fully immerse herself in being there for them.

2011 – In the fall of 2011, my wife's father was up for re-election for the City Council in our hometown. He ran a solid campaign and had successfully been voted in for the past four terms (16 years). This year the outcome would not fall in his favor. My wife went to our hometown on Election Day for her father. She traveled from Rochester to Auburn, New York, alone. She had put in some personal time and effort in support of her father's re-election campaign. She had also been diligently focused on our two boys and her own health.

And then less than a week later in mid-November 2012, after the busyness of the fall, including Aileen's return to teaching when the campaign season ended, all seemed to quiet down. Then right before the ramp-up of the holiday season, Aileen's sight in her right eye contained a black area impairing vision in her right eye that that was rapidly growing to the point where she could not see. Thinking it was nothing serious, she waited through the weekend to go to the doctors. The delay to see a doctor proved detrimental. By the following Monday, everything went black in Aileen's right eye. We went to an optometrist and spent what felt like hours in exam room after exam room, test after test. Everything that could be wrong seemed to be ruled out. The optometrist spoke with me several times during the day, and in each instance his tone seemed to be getting more serious and consolatory. Aileen expressed a myriad of emotions throughout the process. And I did my best to comfort her during a situation that seemed to have no answers.

The doctor finally ruled that the issue with Aileen's sight had nothing to do with the eye, but with the optical nerves that attach to the back of the eye. He recommended a neurologist that she should visit right away, and we shifted gears to another doctor. Fast forward a series of steroid treatments, several neurologist visitations, more eye exams, blood tests, and an MRI, and it was determined based upon the body of information from data, images, and text results that Aileen had Multiple Sclerosis (MS). We were shocked, scared, and confused. We both went through a period of withdrawal, fear, and stress that quite frankly we had ever gone through before in our lives together or independently and were not prepared to manage. But as more doctors' appointments were made and we learned more about the disease and Aileen's specific condition, we slowly began to take back a sense of control that had been lost. This took time. I did my best to support Aileen in every way that I knew how.

When loved ones go through these kinds of events, they often look to their partner to be their "rock," for unconditional support. I believe I did fine but know I could have done better. When a loved one goes through so much shock, pain, and crisis it is challenging to pull out of the chaotic convergence of emotion, data, and uncertainty to fully address their needs. And with two young boys also in need of daily attention, the challenge was great.

Time may heal all things. For those with MS, time feels like a double-edged sword. Living with MS brings with it a high degree of ambiguity, uncertainty and risks associated with Aileen's long-term health and quality of life. The idea of how she will be impacted across time is as frightening as the reality that we must face in the present.

MS is an autoimmune disease two to three times more common in woman than in men. According to the National Multiple Sclerosis Society, approximately 400,000 people in the US have MS, and 200 more people are diagnosed every week. It is also estimated that MS affects more than 2.1 million people worldwide. Epidemiologists, the scientists who study patterns of MS, believe that certain factors appear to be characteristic of who gets MS including: gender, genetics, age, geography, and ethnic background.

MS has been a widely researched disease. However, after more than 140 years of research, there remains no known cause or cure for MS. Scientists have developed treatments that for some patients may slow the progression of MS and may manage certain symptoms. But no one singular treatment is effective for all patients. MS can literally manifest within each individual patient differently, thereby also contributing to symptoms and quality of life impacts that vary for each person who lives with the disease. The illness is also highly unpredictable, leaving those who have MS to always have a certain amount of anxiety over a health issue that they cannot, with the current state of science, fully cure or truly control.

2015 – Lightness begins to shine in. Five years after being diagnosed with ovarian cancer Aileen is doing well and is cancer free. She has regular check-ins with her MS doctor and annual MRIs to determine if there have been any new lesions that have formed in her brain or spine. She takes medicine for MS to try to suppress the growth of new lesions. The medicine is delivered by a shot (needle) that is delivered through the upper thigh. The medicine has side effects and typically makes her feel like she has the flu for half a day to a full day after the shot is administered.

The weekly ritual of administering the shot is something she has had to build into her life. It has become a routine and one that she has never take for granted. What I mean is that here is a woman who had to stick herself with a long needle, once a week, and then go through flu-like symptoms for an entire day—all on purpose! That purpose obviously is life-critical. The medicine is an inhibitor, working to mitigate the advancement of new lesions and the buildup of plaque in her brain and spinal cord. Believe me, this weekly procedure is not something most people ever want to do to themselves. However, Aileen gets it done without complaint or resistance, with the help of her dear cousin, a trained nurse, who has been an incredible support to our family.

Since 2012, Aileen and Owen have had numerous health concerns. Honestly, this book would turn into a long biography if I were to embellish it more with the daily realities or the occasional scares. My wife and I have ridden in the back of an ambulance with my son to SUNY Upstate Medical Center more than once. Aileen has had stretches of good health combined with the terrible moments experiencing MS flares and relapses. These experiences take a toll on the individual and on the family unit going through them. In our experience, it takes a great deal of patience, communication, kindness, and love to stay mentally strong for one another. The irony of life is that none of us has ultimate control.

Like a flick of a switch life can dramatically change, and even end. Yet many of us go about our day with a sense of certainty and comfort in knowing that we have control over many things. However, when your life swiftly changes and you feel like your freefalling without a parachute, you fight for control as if you are gasping for air and dear life itself. I know that feeling all too well, although I, myself, am not one of the persons in our family who has had a disease and gone through the dark abyss of trying to find certainty within the unknown. I can say in the past ten years I have had times when I fought and clawed for control only to realize the harder I fought the more I was losing.

Moreover, the more that I was losing, the more we all were losing. I wanted and still want, dearly, to change the realities of Aileen and Owen's health situations. This story is not about me though. It is about Aileen, Owen, and millions of other people who are suffering, scared, and need unconditional love and support.

Everyone on Earth is tested at some point of his or her existence. Some of us are tested directly, others indirectly. For some, the test is physical; for others it is emotional and psychological. Yet for others it is a test of will and spirituality. How we choose to serve, that is, how we choose to respond to life as it happens ultimately defines our character (who we are and who we will become). It takes profound courage, faith, and conviction to surrender ourselves to the abyss of the unknown.

The five-year period from 2008 through 2013 is a time of my life that seems almost unbelievable. Aileen birthed our two sons. She also had a miscarriage. During this time she was diagnosed with ovarian cancer, lost 90 percent of her vision in her left eye, and was diagnosed with Multiple Sclerosis (MS). During these five years we also determined that our son Owen had the perfect storm of autoimmune diseases including severe food allergies, ulcerative colitis, eosinophilic esophagitis (EE), very bad asthma, and eczema.

We also discovered that he had learning delays and motor skill challenges that required one-on-one personal attention from specialists in speech and physical therapy and from sessions with nutritionists. During these five years, we spent an enormous amount of time visiting with medical specialists and doctors, going in and out of emergency rooms, and spending several days or week-long stints checked in at the regional hospital for the medical care of both Aileen and Owen. The five years were so intensive that my wife and I both joke about our PTSD when strong emotions are triggered by little things we both remember from our experiences. As an example, I will suddenly remember how colicky Owen was. He ALWAYS wanted to be held and rocked. He preferred laying across your arms and moved side to side while you stood. For some reason that motion would calm him down. Our mantra was "keep the motion" . . . or let's just say it was "Never, never stop moving!"

His cry was a shriek, and as much as people love their first-born baby, when that baby has colic, this can bring on post-traumatic stress disorder. I used to rock Owen in a chair for what felt like hours. Ninety percent of the time, it was an enjoyable experience, even if he was crying and angry. Some of the time he would be so uncomfortable that you would just cringe. My body would tighten up so much that it would ache for days. I would sit rocking, with one leg extended and the other pushing the chair back and forth. My right ankle and lower leg muscles would tighten up from the tension of the constant movement. It was months later when I began to realize that my right leg always ached, a constant pain that was a direct result of the intense rocking.

When I reflect on that five-year span of time, I simply do not know how we got through it. Our situation felt surreal, to the point where I stopped talking about it with peers and family. There was a point during this time when I would go to work and my colleagues would ask about this or that, and I would frequently have a new situation to tell them about. They would look at me with utter bewilderment, and I do not blame them. Our experience was almost impossible to believe. Here was a family, and one remarkable woman, who had to reconcile her mortality with being a young mother. She dealt with the emotional and physical difficulties of managing cancer while being diagnosed with a long-term dilapidating disease. She had to heal herself and her son at the same time. The shear amount of strength and personal will power in this woman is simply profound.

There were critical times during those five years, and since then, that she of all people has been my rock and reality-check when "life's got me down." I am embarrassed and ashamed to admit this, but it is true. I did support Aileen the best that I knew how. So much was new to us—having young children, experiencing cancer and MS, and managing a child with severe food allergies. We have been through a lot together and I have tried my best to be there for her in every part of this incredible journey. I know, because I witnessed it firsthand, that there were times when she braved the darkness alone.

We all have to face our mortality at some point. However, doing it in your 30s, alone, and in the face of bringing children into the world, is something I would not wish upon anyone. It is interesting when I think about the sixty months between 2008 and 2013 now. There were and remain so many amazing and beautiful moments. The birth of our sons. Watching them walk for the first time and say their first words. Seeing Aileen joyously become a mom and then so bravely fight cancer and manage MS. These years were not an endless abyss of negativity. Rather, they ended up being a time of tremendous courage and triumph in the face of great challenges.

Since being diagnosed with cancer and MS, Aileen has refocused her energies on herself, her family, and how she wants to spend her time in the world. It is not that she wasn't focused on these aspects of life before. She was. But now much of the minutia and details that consumed and clouded her thoughts have faded. She continues to feel a tug-of-war between professional and personal identity, but not as much as she once did. She has discovered that living life with a sense of purpose and strength comes from within, and that true happiness is an outcome of who she is inside. She is focused on her personal health, wellness, and spirituality. And in this inward and reflective process she is rediscovering her identity and how she will choose to reinsert herself into the world as a stronger, healthier, and happier person. In short, Aileen has chosen to be accountable first and foremost to her! And in the process all else in her life will align with her spirit and greatness.

In conversations with Aileen and others I have learned that, for many, having a disease was a catalyst for reevaluating their life to recalibrate their role in the world, and to refocus how they make the most of each day. It is so easy for any of us to get caught up in the details and complexities of daily life that we often forget what is important, including who our true "self" is.

Working parents, and working mothers in particular, focus so intently on being responsible and accountable to everyone in their universe: husbands, children, teachers, colleagues, coworkers, friends, family, and parents. Yet what often gets overlooked is the need to be accountable to one's self.

The experiences of these five years were incredibly difficult for our family, and they changed me personally. They also changed Aileen in some fundamental ways. Today, she sees life with a greater sense of clarity and urgency than before. She understands the limitations of time (on Earth), and the true need for kindness, dignity, and resolve to be present in all relations. On the back end of this deep life experience, we have become closer, stronger, and better together. This is not to say we did not have some very tough times and low points. But at our core as a couple, we respect ourselves, we respect each other, and we respect our relationship. That foundation has weathered us through any hardship we have encountered, from financial stress to raising a child with disabilities to facing disease and death head-on. We chose a life together, and together we are choosing to thrive in the face of any adversity that comes our way.

On Dignity and Love

I believe human dignity exists when people are unencumbered by the weight of others (meaning other people's beliefs, actions, emotions, perceptions, judgments,and so forth) and are able to reach for and attain their greatest potential by becoming their highest self. Humans have a visceral human need for belonging, identity, influence, self-preservation, and growth. When any of these needs are unmet or constrained, we can fail to establish our dignity.

Dignity is what binds us together, through thick and thin, good times and bad. It is the sticky factor and source code of our human existence. Dignity occurs when people live as individuals, freely and openly, to express themselves in a world of possibility. Of course, there are moral frameworks, governments, religion, policies, and laws that set boundary conditions for keeping us safe, secure, and within our rights as citizens. However, having dignity is something deeper than these social constructs that humans design.

Dignity is the base code that exists within us, in the absence of rules, regulations, policies, and even religion. It exists where the unconscious and consciousness of human existence come together.

Dignity is the recognition that we all have a soul, and that each of our souls are precious and unique. While we all look different on the outside, we all share a common connection in space, in time, and the Universe. Our dignity binds us across the immeasurable reaches of space and time. Dignity is what makes humans conscious beings, aware of our thoughts, and with cognitive abilities that allow us to contemplate space, time, and experiences beyond what we can sense from the physical world.

The human experience is very much a shared one. I personally believe we occupy Earth for only a brief slice of our soul's existence. As an intelligent species, humans inherently and intuitively understand and explore love. Love is a manifestation of dignity, expressed in many forms. The sheer fact that humans seek out and provide unconditional love is a reflection of our shared dignity. Think about when we use phrases like "I love you to the moon and back," or "I will love you for infinity." We express feelings in such a way not because we are extravagant or unrealistic, but because somewhere deep down inside us, we know that love can be everlasting, and that at its core it is universal and omnipresent, lighting our souls in birth, life, death, and beyond.

Consider the institution of marriage and the fact that two people commit themselves fully to each other, without any clarity or certainty of the future, to hold true to the sanctity of their vows, "until death do us part." The sanctity of marriage is a human expression of shared dignity. It is the purest form of partnership that says, no matter what goes down from here on out, I have your back. That is a bold promise to make and commitment to uphold. Think about how many people are not committed to their workout routine, their job, or their friends and family. It is easy for people to walk away from human dignity out of selfishness or because they are unable to find certainty in those deeds or relations.

The hard truth about dignity is that it is not only about what we receive from others, it is also about what we give, how we serve, and when we choose to give others their space and time. Dignity is not all about us! It is the soul's reflection in another, mirroring and signaling love, comfort, restraint, and compassion. When we give ourselves fully to something or somebody, for example in marriage, we willingly choose to express our dignity for ourselves and for them. Thus dignity is mirrored; it is shared. Our dignity is about treating all forms of life fairly, with mutual respect.

May the "Dignity" Force Be with You

It was a typical workweek evening. After dinner, my two boys finished their homework, had a snack and chilled out for a few minutes before a bath and then bedtime. We went through the motions with precision, like a well-oiled machine, doing our nightly routine.

When it came to bedtime my wife and I tag-teamed helping our two boys brush their teeth and get settled into bed. I read a short story to our youngest son. As we read the story, we both could hear the older brother crying from his room. He was telling his mom a story and sobbing. The older brother was in the best hands possible, so I let mom take care of the situation. The youngest son wanted to check on his big brother and said he hoped he was okay. I provided him with assurance that he would be fine and that mom was helping him.

My older son cried for a few more minutes, and then settled down. I finished the story with our youngest, who then fell sleep.

I tucked him in and went to check in on my wife and his brother. She said he was upset and overtired. She told me he told he felt frightened by some of his toy Star Wars and other figurines that seemed to "come to life" and scared him. The thought of Kylo Ren and Chewbacca figurines coming alive freaked me the hell out also, so I could see how that would weigh on the imaginative 9-year-old mind before bedtime.

My wife said when she was a child she used to have similar thoughts of inanimate toys coming to life. I thought, "ha" there it was, at least for this specific situation. This family gene was passed down to my son from her, not me. Then I thought how silly that was, since it was not bad to be fearful of the mind playing tricks on us. Heck, when I walk through our house I believe I see things moving out of the corner of my eye that are not there. Or are they?

At any rate, I got the intel from my wife and then went into my older son's room to see how he was doing and whether he had fallen asleep. As I entered the room, I couldn't help looking toward his desk and shelf area where Kylo Ren was last spotted fighting an epic Star Wars battle with Luke Skywalker, Rey, Boba Fett, and Darth Maul. As I glanced at the figures through the dimly lit bedroom they did not appear to make ghastly faces at me or turn their heads around 360 degrees and spit out green soup. I felt relieved.

So I proceeded to my son's bed. Before I could look down to see if his eyes were open or closed I heard him say, "Hey, dad." I replied, "Hey, how are you doing?" My son asked, "Can I tell you something?" I said, "Of course, what is it?"

As I sat beside him in his bed, I began to prepare my thoughts, thinking about "what mom would say." I expected my son to talk about how the figurine toys in his room were scary at night, as he had a few minutes earlier with his mom. But there was no mention of Star Wars figures, toys, or anything in the room or in the house for that matter. What my son said next actually disturbed and worried me, mostly because I did not have an appropriate answer prepared, let alone one that I could craft and distill into 9-year-old language on the fly before bedtime.

With the covers pulled up under his chin, my son calmly yet firmly stated, "Dad, there are a lot of negative people around." I was, for a moment, dumbfounded. Expecting to talk about the evil nature of toys in the dark, I was perplexed. Where was this thought coming from? I asked my son what he meant. He added, "A lot of negative things are happening in the world right now. There are bad people and bad things everywhere." Thinking that he may be magnifying something that has happened during his school day I asked, "Is everything okay at school?" He said it was, but some of his classmates were "negative" and "said bad things about the world ending and people dying," and so on.

After a sequence of answers to my questions trying to get to the root cause of his emotions, I realized he was internalizing a combination of experiences and observations about his day at school and the general state of affairs in the world.

As parents, my wife and I have tried to shield our two boys from the doom and gloom of the 24/7 news cycle. We do not have CNN streaming in the background, and we try to alleviate negative dialog, behaviors, and thinking from our daily life. It was clear on this evening that our son was harboring strong feelings about negative people in the world. He told me more about how the world "going in the wrong direction." Speaking in a low voice but with an eerily emphatic tone, he then said, "I'm going to change the world . . . I have my speech all in my head . . . someday I will give the speech to my class."

It may have been the fact that it was bedtime, or the fact that the room was dark, and that I was likely overtired from a long day. But when my son spoke those words of conviction as he lay tucked tightly into his bed, I could not help feeling a little emotional about this myself. Here was a child, speaking 100 percent from his heart about the stark realities of the world that can be cold and dark, negative and sinister. He could have said any of a million things, but his conclusion was that he felt things were "heading in the wrong direction" and that he wanted to do something about it. He wanted to be a force for good and change. He wanted to speak his mind and influence others to stop being negative. My son was nine years old.

Let us all pause to think about this for a moment. Today a lot of data, information, and change bombards youth in America and around the world. What they experience in their schools, communities, homes, and through social media is, directly and indirectly, influencing their minds, personalities, and behaviors. No matter how much we might want to shield and protect our kids, they are being exposed to many influences that also infiltrate and impact their peers, parents, teachers, doctors, coaches, and caregivers.

There is an epic battle raging throughout the world and ravaging our society. The battle was magnified in recent years by the speed by which data and information (fact or fiction) is instantaneously exchanged on global scale by the push of a button. The amount of damage 280 characters can do is really quite alarming. The proverbial "finger on the button" isn't so much about nuclear warfare anymore; it is rather the ability to have mass amounts of people essentially "go nuclear" following a misguided Tweet.

In the past, the battleground lines used to be geographic and physical, enabling things like fortified walls to be constructed or for Armies to be strategically stationed. With definitive battleground lines, children can be kept safe and sheltered from the rhetoric that rousts and rallies people to the front lines. However, today the battlefield is less about boundaries of geography and physical might, and more about emotion, perception, deception, and what lurks in the deep web and shadows of data, privacy, and subterfuge. As parents we don't even know what it means to parent in this kind of asymmetric world bordering on a dystopian future.

The front lines are no longer a world away. The war is being waged in our schools, homes, and during nighttime talks before bedtime. The epic battle I speak of is complex and has made billions of dollars for theme parks, Hollywood, multinational defense companies, and the United States and foreign governments.

George Lucas brilliantly captured the basic tenet and existential nature of the battle in the *Star Wars* trilogy. The battle before us, thousands of years in the making, and our greatest threat, is that between good versus evil. I hate to say it is that simple, but it is. As my son's *Star Wars* characters manned the front lines of his shelf, I put my arm around him, hugging him firmly. I ran my fingers through his hair, and told him that he had an enormous heart, a beautiful soul, and has already changed the world for the better.

Dignity comes in many forms. It can be shared, expressed, felt, performed, and received. The battle between good and evil can only be won and eradicated when we all choose, like my son, to push away the darkness and embrace the light.

Ridding Our Lives of Negative Thinking and Behavior

It's amazing and sobering how the unfiltered and unbiased voice and action of a child can keep you in check and even change your life.

On a cold and damp morning in early March, six words from my son seemed to annihilate my very being, shattering my self-concept and reminding me of the critical importance that integrity and personal accountability play in each moment of every day.

On this morning, as the coffee dripped and a heavy rain poured, my mind was flooded with my day's to-do list: Bring the kids to school by 8:35 a.m., get back in time for a 9:00 a.m. teleconference, finish a proposal by noon, meet a business colleague at 12:30 p.m., call in some prescriptions, pay a couple of bills, edit an article sitting at my desk for too long, stop at the grocery store, and something else I knew I was forgetting.

I glanced at the coffee pot and was momentarily mesmerized by the blissful image of sipping on a fresh cup . . . Five minutes of organically brewed caffeinated serenity before the first call of the day . . .

"Daddy, can I have more orange juice?" my youngest boy, a spirited five-year-old, piped up. Snapped back to reality from my mental oasis, I immediately fetched the OJ. His brother put in an additional request for some more breakfast as I navigated the kitchen with the swiftness of a short-order cook. Keep in mind that precision is essential in the morning.

I was fully immersed in Phase 1 of Operation Get the Kids to School on Time. My head was foggy. I felt the morning fluster as I fielded requests from my boys. A flurry of competing demands floated around in my mind.

There are three phases of this operation, in case you were wondering:

Phase 1 is satisfying the pleading and feeding.

Phase 2 is getting them clean and clothed.

Phase 3 is making the on-time drop at school.

Now there are nuanced subtleties to all these phases. For example, in Phase 1 of breakfast, you also have to make lunches, get school bags organized, and make sure homework is done.

Maybe more organized people drink their hot coffee as they get their kids ready. Perhaps people with more discipline get up earlier in the morning than I do. Both are logical options, but have yet to pan out for me, or for my wife, I might add. We're morning procrastinators—you know, the kind of people that play cat-and-mouse with the iPhone alarm snooze button until one of us wakes up gasping for air, arms flailing about, trying to temper a potential aneurysm or heart attack. The ability to jump out of bed with the ferocity of an awakened Grizzly and immediately make sense of one's surroundings is a downright talent.

"Eat up, boys. Then let's wash our hands, brush our teeth, and get clothes on for school." I said. I could sense my boys, even at ages five and seven, rolling their eyes and saying politely "yeah, yeah, okay dad," as if they hadn't heard this line a thousand times.

Suddenly I noticed the two bags of trash near the back door. I remembered it was trash day! And, of course, it was raining outside! All mornings, especially school days, are hectic. But for some reason, trash day seems to greatly magnify the frenzy. There are trash days when it is picked up very early and then those when the pick-up is later in the afternoon. I've never been able to figure out the schedule. But instead of playing a game of trash-roulette with what time the waste hauler will arrive, I've decided to put out the trash first thing in the morning before the boys go to school. This is likely a male-based fixation, but for whatever reason I've stuck with it.

As the coffee dripped in unison with the second hand of the clock, my entire existence felt as if it were being mocked. Isn't it amazing how quickly time seems to pass when pressed for time and sits still when you are anticipating the future? Somehow thirty minutes flashed as if they were thirty seconds. We were now flirting with the fine line between being right on time or late to school. Right on time would mean the boys had to finish up breakfast quickly and head upstairs where mom would help them complete Phase 2 of Operation Get the Kids to School on Time.

With affirmation, I spoke up, "I will be right back. I'm taking out the trash. Please head upstairs so mommy can get you ready." As I picked up the bags and opened the door, I let out a selfish wail of frustration, "uhg, grr, stupid trash, blah blah, cold, wet, nasty, don't need this, blah blah." I don't remember the exact phrases of verbal drivel, but it was the tone that was significant. Kids pick up on tone and temperament as much, if not more, than the actual words.

I stepped off the back porch and proceeded up the driveway. The trash containers are conveniently located behind the detached garage, maybe 30 yards from the house. On a sunny and relaxed day, the walk is great. Smell the spring air . . . hear those birds chirping . . . feel the warm rays of the sun upon your face . . . but not on this day. Needles of mixed precipitation shot down and stung my face as if I were being blasted by a water gun. As I marched from sidewalk to driveway, I thought about the next five tasks needing to be accomplished to successfully complete Operation Get the Kids to School on Time.

No sooner did my feet hit the driveway when I heard the back-door swing open. The next sequence of events felt almost mystical, isolated within time. I swung my head and looked over my shoulder. My five-year old, dressed in his pajamas, stepped out on the wet porch. He looked out at me and shouted, "C'mon daddy, you're better than that!" He then turned around and ran inside the house.

For a millisecond, I was perplexed, unsure of what my son was trying to say. Then it hit me like a ton of trash. I let out a hearty laugh. When real truths are spoken, they can have a profound impact on one's emotions. In this instance, my release was laughter. The frustration I felt, fighting the time pressure and all caught up with this in my head, immediately lifted. My son's words, innocent and honest, hit my heart and jugular like a dagger. My son had reacted to my raw emotions. He was right; I am better than that. Why was I so caught up in my mind with my anxieties? Why did I not see my negative emotions and, worse, why did I not prevent myself from revealing this? After all, I'm the adult, and should have been behaving like one.

I took the trash to the curb and then drove the car down the driveway. A few minutes later my sons came out, all dressed and ready for school. As they hopped inside, I helped my youngest with his seatbelt. I looked him in the eyes and said, "Thank you, you're right. Daddy is better than that. I'm sorry for acting so frustrated." He looked at me and said, "It's okay, Dad. I just want you to be happy."

* * *

Happy. A simple word that describes one of the deepest emotions and behaviors humans can have. Happiness can be attained, but more often than not it is a deliberate choice we have to make.

Negativity is insidious, and it likes company. That's why negative emotions are often worn on one's sleeve to selfishly draw in an audience to let them know you are in pain and frustrated. But the self-centered martyr seeking attention pushes others away, ultimately manifesting a reality marked by undesirable relationships and loneliness. When the ego thrives on negativity, one's reality is rewarded in kind with a negative reality.

I'm guilty of moments in my life when my best self was subdued by a negative ego seeking spectators. I'm ashamed that my son felt the need to shake me up to awaken my higher sense of self. I'm also quite embarrassed to share this story openly. But as someone who believes deeply in personal integrity, accountability, and trust, I believe it's necessary for me to not only learn from my experiences but to open up and share them as well.

Consider the relationships you have and who you believe you are as a person versus how others may perceive you. Ask yourself, "Do I present myself in my highest sense of self, aiming for the utmost integrity and dignity?" How can I direct this through my character in all that I do? Can I be a positive influence and role model for my children, my spouse, or my friends and community?

I often think about my son's words and how they influenced me. I'm certainly not perfect by any measure. I just know that the most important things, such as love, relationships, and life itself are diminished when we allow ourselves to propagate negative behaviors. Whenever I sense myself sliding down the slippery slope of ego-driven negativity, I think of the back door swinging open and seeing my son's beautiful face emerge, and hearing his enlightened words, "C'mon daddy, you're better than that!"

6

Reframing Your State of Mind

A few years ago, I was taking a flight from Rochester, New York, to Tucson, Arizona, to attend an environmental business conference I was asked to speak at. I recall the trip vividly since it was about nine months before the formal publication of *The Sustainability Generation*. My talk was about "Developing the Next Generation of EHS (Environment, Health and Safety) Leaders through Strategic Succession Planning."

That topic was a mouthful. But I was basically asked to speak about the emerging skills, capabilities, characteristics, traits, values, and behaviors of "next generation" environmental business leaders. The conference committee was interested in where the industry of environmental management was moving and, with it, the types of talent needed for success.

The conference and talk went splendidly. I was able to deliver my presentation and engage in a panel dialogue in a meaningful way. The experience enabled me to bring forth some key concepts and topics from *The Sustainability Generation* before an audience of peers, further helping me to refine and clarify my core message. One of the key areas of dialog for the panel and the audience that day was around the stark differences in culture, work ethic, and values between boomers and millennials. The audience was mostly made up of mid-career and older professionals. It became clear to me that I was one of the younger people in the room, presenting a talk on a topic that most of the audience had led a career experiencing, and on a topic that was super charged with emotion, perception, and fear.

The emotion was transparent and reflective of the fact that most of the boomers (those born between 1946 and 1964) in the room expressed deep frustration about working beside millennials (the Gen Ys born between 1982 and 2004), whom they felt were unprepared for the workforce. The perception was that millennials, as a generation of workers, were lazy, entitled, selfish, and unrealistic about their career. The underlying fear shared by boomers was that millennials may actually have some form of an edge on the older generation when it came to technology, data analytics, and the ability to assimilate data and information into meaningful metrics, reports, and narrative—skills that in an age of information and digital transformation could make their generation obsolete.

As I listened to the audience talk about their relationship (or lack thereof) with millennials it was clear to me that their perceptions were shaped more by fear than by truth. I challenged the group by telling them they were all early career professionals at one time in their life and may have had similar perceptions placed upon them by their supervisors twenty and thirty years ago. I asked them to visualize their early-career and picture who they were at that time of their life. I then asked them to think about who they had become in their career and if it measured up to the image they had of themselves when they were in their early 20s.

The look of consternation could be seen on many of the faces in the audience. It was clear that many of them were beginning to see that how they thought about their career in their early 20s was much different from how they were thinking about it at our meeting. I then asked the audience a sequence of questions about leadership and challenged them to think about where they were in their careers—not competing with millennials, but empowering and leading them to drive performance in the business enterprise—as well as mentoring them to lead fuller and richer lives.

The audience began shifting in their seats. The looks of dread began to lift and facial expressions began to emulate hope, confidence, and joy. Many people in the audience began to reframe who they were. Instead of thinking of their jobs as competitive and "on the chopping blocks" they said that they have led meaningful careers with diverse experiences. As a result, they had unparalleled context, knowledge, understanding and insight into not only their job but also their entire corporation, business sector, and global economy. Furthermore, they understood that they had an opportunity, should they choose to pursue it, to not just manage people but to mentor and lead them. This minor tweak in mindset that shifted their negative thinking, elevated the mood and aspirations of the audience.

While not everyone may have walked away from the presentation with a newfound focus on leadership, I'm confident a few did and then took it upon themselves to stop viewing the younger generation as a force of competitive tension, but instead as a force for good that needed to be harnessed, guided, and directed.

No matter where you are in life, there is always a unique role for you to serve. We should not fear what we do not fully understand. We do not want to operate our life (or livelihood) based upon misguided or false assumptions. I advise that you challenge yourself and the status quo of your peers. You can reinvent yourself by reframing your capabilities, strengths, and goals in a new context that will reshape your reality here and now and into the future.

We should not succumb to those that want to bring us down to the level of their limited beliefs, behaviors, and perceptions of the world. Some reject change at every chance they get, as they themselves fear change and would rather go without having it imposed on them than become leaders who accept the occurrence of change and choose to create a new future because they fear what is ahead.

There is much to embrace about what is going on in your career and in your organization, community, and home. Be a voice that is driving forward, not one that is set on pointing the finger at generation-next as the reason your career (or life) has not advanced as you had intended.

REDEFINING YOUR STATE OF MIND

Food for Thought: Real Inclusion Requires Self-Awareness, Compassion, Creativity, and Flexibility

My son has severe food allergies. For nine years my wife and I have ridden the emotional food-allergy roller coaster. During most of this time, our son has been strapped tightly into the seat of the roller coaster, sitting safely between us. However, as he has grown to into a vibrant third grader, we feel as if we are helplessly watching our son bounce around in the first seat of the roller coaster as we watch in horror from the back. Feeling fraught with fear, my wife and I continue to reconcile how we can keep our child safe amid the sharp twists, gut-wrenching turns, and stomach dropping zero gravity loops of protecting a child with food allergies.

Statistics show that autoimmune diseases are on the rise. In fact, autoimmune diseases affect more than 50 million Americans, or nearly one in five people. People and the lives they lead represent much more than numbers however. Our son, who is severely allergic to all dairy (milk), eggs, peanuts and tree nuts, soy, and certain types of melons, carries an EpiPen with him at all times, a life-saving drug to be administered should he have an anaphylactic reaction. He is also moderately allergic to carrots, corn, and varieties of other berries and vegetables. Our son also has chronic eczema, asthma, and colitis. A couple of years ago he was diagnosed with eosinophilic esophagitis (EE).

According to Food Allergy Research and Education[38] (FARE), there are more than 15 million Americans with food allergies. FARE states that one in thirteen children in the United States (or approximately two children in every classroom) have food allergies and are at risk, like our son, for life-threatening anaphylaxis. Public awareness of food allergies is increasing, thanks to the efforts of advocacy organizations including FARE.

This is good news, particularly for parents of children with food allergies who constantly find themselves dividing their time between ensuring their child's dietary needs are met (safe and nutritious foods), while simultaneously educating other people who come into contact with their child.

Lisa Gable, CEO of FARE states, "Learning you or a loved one has a life-threatening disease has a life-altering impact. Medical management follows the diagnosis, but an often overlooked aspect of living with a complex disease is the emotional toll that families experience as a result of navigating issues of safety, inclusion and lack of understanding. Empathy is the missing element."

For many parents and children alike, the arduous uphill and daily battle to manage food allergies is exacerbated by people who are simply unwilling to shift their beliefs, attitudes, behaviors, or pride—particularly on something as personal as food. Unfortunately, for most people, unless something directly affects them personally, they will not expend too much energy or effort trying to empathize or understand the needs of others.

Humans (and Americans in particular) have a profound and emotional relationship with our food. We love food. Whether fast and friendly, or fresh from the farm, our follies about food are abundant and have come to define who we are by what we eat. As human have evolved, so too has our relationship with food.

Our relationship with food is complex and personal. People love to talk about (and be praised for) food as much as they love to eat it. That best recipe for chili that gets rave reviews every time. Those tantalizing Thanksgiving Day leftover mashups. The scrumptious slice of strawberry cheesecake that reminds you of your first "going out" Valentine's date. It is no wonder we love food. Food is like that best friend who has been with us through every life experience, to support us, comfort us, and give us pleasure (and sometimes pain). Food is our BFF! High-Five! Yeah!

At its most raw and basic function, food provides us with nourishment and energy so that we can live healthy, productive, and happy lives. That aspect of the human-food relationship is the most essential. Today, however, food is so much more than sustenance. Food is emotional, inextricably melding our conscious and subconscious mind in a state of euphoria. We have come to make food less about our health and nutritional requirements and more about our emotional response to external factors including:

- *Positive experiences* (celebrations like birthdays, anniversaries, holidays, etc.)

- *Negative feedback behaviors* (delving deep into that half-gallon of double chocolate brownie ice-cream after that nasty break-up)

- *Social acceptance and connectivity* (eating a few extra chicken wings during the "big game." This is the tribal diet—engaging in foods by virtue of who you hang out with most frequently.)

- *Convenient meal solutions* (buying pizza or fast food because its "easier" than making something in the kitchen after those long days at work)

- *Lifestyle choices* (decisions about eating based on geography, health, diet, wellness, and so on)

Herein lies the issue. We have serious and entrenched behavioral problems with food. Food, per say, is not to blame. People (not burgers) are the problem. When it comes to food, we all have our blinders. While our "food misconduct disorder" is not entirely our fault, it is our responsibility to be self-aware of our behaviors and more importantly, conscious to the needs of those around us.

You have likely heard the saying, "you are what you eat." For children with food allergies the saying is "you are what you don't eat (or touch)." Children with severe food allergies cannot exercise the same luxury, freedoms, or lust for food that people without food allergies can. When people discover that my son has severe food allergies they typically response with "oh my gosh, what can he eat?" or "how terrible, you guys must have to cook a lot" or "so sad that he cannot experience peanut butter or ice-cream." But quite frankly, as parents, the shocking and sad news for my wife and me has been not the raising of a child with food allergies. It is having to continuously create new strategies to educate, inform, and convince grown adults to understand and accept the challenge.

As parents, we put a great deal of trust into the constellation of adults that come in and out of our children's lives each day. So many individuals directly influence our children's life. As parents, we put our faith into grandparents, aunts and uncles, dentists and doctors, teachers and aids, school administrators, crossing guards, bus drivers, school custodians, resource officers, and other parents. We look to these folks as experts in their respective roles, but also as purveyors of logic and common sense when and where issues arise (and they do).

When it comes to food allergies, the majority of time and effort my wife and I spend on keeping our child safe is not one-on-one with him, but in the trust-building with everyone else who interfaces with him. Too often we have had to play good cop/bad cop with our families, working to maintain a level of awareness with them, not only about the health and safety aspects of our sons food allergies, but also about the need to ensure he feels (and truly is) included in family activities, so many of which often revolve around food. Food and family are like bees and honey, Adele and the Grammys, peanut butter and jelly, or Cinderella and the glass slipper. That is to say, food and family are inseparable; they really like each other.

Now go to a family function, say a birthday party, and try to tell everyone that it's insensitive to have ice-cream because one of the kids at the party cannot partake because of his allergies. Believe me, that Pandora's Box will open, giving rise to Lucifer himself cloaked in black, flying a fire-breathing dragon, and swinging his sword fiercely in front of your cart on the roller coaster. Deep from the bellows of his once dormant gut, the most judgmental question-statement reverberates through the air, blowing back your hair, "You mean just lactose intolerant, don't you?! . . . we can still serve the ice-cream, perhaps he (our son) can just wait in the other room until we finish."

Major holidays, birthdays, celebrations, summertime picnics and reunions, and a host of other family oriented activities are tough on individuals with food allergies. Just as challenging are the school-related activities where peers are involved. My wife and I have found that kids tend to be very empathetic, caring, and responsive to their peers with food allergies (or other health challenges). On the contrary, adults are more rigid in their thinking and less willing to break behaviors for the safety and well-being of one student.

In too many instances to recall, parents and teachers have resorted to maintaining a "status-quo" in how functions with food are carried out, mostly because their ego, pride, or emotional-blinders prevented them seeing the one child for his particular needs. We have encountered Valentine's Day parties where the heart-shaped dairy frosted cookies "just had to be" a part of the occasion and the fall "apple day" celebration that included vanilla ice cream "because that's how they always served the warm apples the kids made." Well neither occasion showed respect let alone love to the child who could not be included in those activities due to his allergies.

Frequently we make situations about us when they really they should be about the person who is really affected. In the case of my son, the conversation typically goes to food and safety, but rarely ties into what he perceives, is thinking, or likes or doesn't like. Of course, health and safety is our #1 priority as a parent of a child with food allergies. As our son matures, it is also critical that he is included in classroom activities and perceived as an equal by his peers. Health can be skin deep; however, matters of the heart drive emotional growth and total wellness. Children with severe food allergies know that they are different. They carry a lifesaving drug with them at all times to remind them of that reality.

Separating our love affair with food from the real-life challenges of people all around us is not hard. Yes, we will have to challenge convention (and in some cases family or community tradition), revamp the menus with allergy friendly foods, and put the pressure on everyone washes their hands before and after they eat. With a little self-awareness, creativity, and compassion we can move beyond the behaviors that drive our food fixations and focus more on what matters, that one child whose spirit has been broken, not by food, but by food lovers that have been unwilling to bend just a little.

Allow Dignity to Flourish: Develop Your Medium of Self-Expression[39]

Humanity is undergoing an alarming crisis of lack of trust and human dignity. Pompous politicians, hidden hackers, and irresponsible executives are unfortunately actively shaping our world this very moment. They are unapologetic as they put forces of fear and coercion to use as weapons of manipulation, control, and obstruction of truth. Often these "weapons" are masked within political rhetoric that is working to undermine progress by pitting humans against ourselves.

Apathetic to the fate of humanity, these fear mongers are willing to forego any sense of the greater good for their own personal vengeance, political or economic gain, or sheer ego. Perhaps most disturbing is the fact that greater society sometimes falls victim to allowing the self-destructive behaviors and tactics of a few to permeate our own beliefs and values, leading to a state of our perpetual distrust. When this happens, we all fail.

Ultimately, humans' ability to survive and thrive resides in our capacity to embrace a common dignity for all living things. The Achilles heel for humanity is how we treat ourselves, each other, and the world around us. But if we cannot take care of each other, how can we possibly serve as caretakers of the earth, this vast expanse of land and water resources that enable our very existence?

Sustainability is not only about environmental conservation or mitigating the impacts of climate change. At its core, sustainability is about the human condition and the values, beliefs, and behaviors which define who we are and how we want to be received and treated. In this context, dignity is about discovering and developing the skills necessary for the world to understand us. It is also equally important for us to have the skills to actively listen to and appreciate the "rest of world" and discover how we can productively work together to improve the condition of our collective humanity.

Of late I find myself thinking about the "mediums by which individuals express themselves." Humans are expressive beings. We each have unique personalities and perspectives. I have found that most people struggle not with self-identity so much as with how to best allow their true identity to shine through to the world. That is, how can I express myself fully and completely, without fearing others' prejudice or bias, so that I feel as if I am heard, understood, and appreciated? People communicate in many different ways. Humans place high emphasis on verbal and conversational communication. However, verbal communication is just one of the mediums by which we express ourselves.

While most people express themselves by spoken words, many people are gifted writers or choose to freely express themselves through music, art, dance, sports, fashion, or spirituality. There are many mediums of self-expression, yet we tend to hone in on and place the most emphasis on verbal communication as a primary and ubiquitous medium that everyone should excel at.

The reality is that while some people communicate by speaking very well, most are terrible. Have you ever experienced a day where your brain feels completely detached from your body? As if what you want to say just doesn't seem to break through the neurons and synapses of your mind to create anything sensible to flow out of your mouth and into the ears of those you're trying to communicate with? I know that I've had those days. Those moments seem to occur at the most inopportune moments, like when you are trying your best to express an emotion with a loved one, or when interviewing for a new job, or those times you are trying to communicate a new idea you have to a colleague.

Whenever I am confronted with looks of consternation or other cues that my message is not heard, it can leave me feeling frustrated, if not completely deflated. It takes a lot of energy to communicate well, partly because the thoughts and feelings we project externally are only a piece of the equation. Where a lot of energy should be spent, but often isn't, is in active sensing and listening of others and in careful monitoring of one's thoughts, emotions, and behaviors in response to others.

Some of the happiest people I know are those that consistently and effectively exercise their chosen mediums for communication. For example, I know many authors, musicians, and artists, each of whom relish in communicating through text, music, painting, and sculpture. They communicate by virtue of creating an emotional connection between themselves and others. Their chosen medium of self-expression opens them up to the world in a dynamic way. Whether anyone is actively "listening" (interpreting, reading, watching, engaging), is always the question. Regardless of whether there is an audience, the medium of expression serves an important purpose as a conduit for creation and self-expression, which are innate human needs.

Mediums of self-expression are important for personal fulfillment and achieving success. They sometimes provide a unique voice or platform by which we can be heard. They are also opportunities for others to engage and translate their thoughts, feelings, and emotions in expressive ways.

There is great dignity in many forms of self-expression. Respecting other people's dignified forms of expression is critical to active listening and important for building and maintaining trust. Be mindful of how you and other people choose to communicate, and the mediums by which you feel most engaged and expressive.

You can enrich yourself by exploring new mediums and being open to engaging with others who choose different forms of expression. We should accept the fact that others may not always understand us right out of the gate. We should also accept that others may not always be communicating at their best capacity. When we provide others the necessary patience, space, and respect they can develop their medium of expression. When we find our best mode of communication and can learn from each other, we all flourish.

When we open our eyes to it, there is great abundance of hope and creativity throughout the world. If we choose to see, listen, and understand mediums of others' personal expression, we become attuned to the rich diversity of life and our shared dignity. By more fully understanding and appreciating one another, we can move beyond uncivil rhetoric and work toward a more just, peaceful, and sustainable existence.

Know That The Heart Matters More

I have learned in life that everyone has a heart, but not all people listen or follow their heart. Some people do not like it when others have a "bleeding heart," that is, those that are outspoken for others in need. Yet there are "bleeding hearts" in the world that simply cannot comprehend how some people can be so crass, uncaring and cold to others. At face value, I am of the belief that turning a back to another in need is simply turning your back to love and ultimately to your own sense of self-worth. If you do not value others, how can you possibly truly value yourself deep down and vice-versa? If you do not value yourself, how can you ever provide an open heart and value to another human being?

There are many ways to help others in need. You do not have to be, as some might say, soft-hearted. Make no mistake; a completely hands-off, passive, and ignorant existence will likely yield an empty personal life. At some point, we all have to roll up our sleeves and put in some effort to empower and enrich the lives of those around us, as well as better our own.

A life well spent is not for the meek. Have you ever noticed that those that are the most compliant or complacent "status quo" kind of people are also the ones that complain the most, about everything? Moreover, in many cases these are some of the most narrow-minded, insular, and negative people as well. They complain about the homeless walking the streets and dirtying up the town, yet have never done one thing in their life to change that situation. They look down at someone who wants to try something, almost anything, to effect a change for the better. I am sorry, but we need more people in this world who see the world for what it can become and scream at the top of their lungs to make it so, not for those that see it as it is and gripe about it over a beer and nachos.

Many people may not know of Greg Schiller. But he and his story are inspirational and illustrative to how one bleeding heart and an act of kindness can ultimately mobilize the attention, resources, and will of people to actually start making change for people in dire need, and for people who are in need and don't even know it.

I first heard of Mr. Schiller in January 2018 following a National Public Radio (NPR) news story about a suburban Chicago resident who was offering "slumber parties" to homeless people in his neighborhood to provide them with refuge during severely cold weather.

As the story goes, Mr. Schiller opened the basement of his property up to homeless people from Elgin, a suburb of Chicago, during harsh winter conditions including extreme cold temperatures. Mr. Schiller told news reporters that he would provide coffee and food to the homeless, and that he would stay up all night with them. He indicated no drugs or alcohol would be allowed at his home. Mr. Schiller fashioned his basement into a temporary shelter, providing cots and sleeping bags to those in need.

Unfortunately, government officials in the city of Elgin had to shut down Mr. Schiller's operation when they deemed his residence was not compliant with local building codes related to regulations for adequate ventilation and lighting in his basement. A significant problem was that he was unable to provide basement fire exits. Local law enforcement and city officials believed that while Mr. Schiller was well intentioned, his basement was not the appropriate place to house homeless people and that it actually put him, his residence, and the homeless at undue risk. Mr. Schiller had told reporters that he opened his basement so that homeless would "not freeze to death," particularly when wind chill values were 15 degrees or less. He claimed that although there were shelters in the city, they often were at capacity or did not open until temperatures were very severe.

Mr. Schiller was ultimately told by the local authorities who closed his operation that he was prohibited from having future "slumber parties." They also pointed out that the city has lawful and compliant shelters that were open and suitable for people during harsh weather and winter conditions and in other circumstances of need. But Mr. Schiller's story did not end here. Following the debacle with the local authorities that made national news, Mr. Schiller began to receive investor pledges in support of his cause. In February 2018, the *Chicago Tribune*[40] reported that Mr. Schiller had received $450,000 in pledges to launch a new homeless shelter to provide service to the homeless in Elgin.

With the newfound capital and attention, Mr. Schiller started a new ministry called House of Hope Transitional Living and Support Center, and a new Facebook page had been created called, Hope for the Homeless. According to the *Chicago Tribune* story, Mr. Schiller said a board would be created to govern the shelter and that they would contract with other local nonprofits to support their needs. He envisioned a future where the shelter would provide overnight stays, job training, day programs, drug and alcohol reha-bilitation, GED counseling, a computer center and office space for other area organizations, and other special services.

People who are less fortunate or are in a state of need repre-sent an opportunity to bring peace, joy, love and compassion to them and the world. As individuals, we may not be able to solve for every social, behavioral, medical, environmental, or psychological challenge—especially not at a global scale. But as individuals we can choose to give when we can give, even if it is only a smile at another human and expression of empathy, kindness, and affec-tion to elevate the hope and spirit of others.

This brings me back to the art of war that rages within many of us. This epic battle between good versus evil is brought on not by the grievances we have with humanity at-large, but by the conflict which lies within ourselves. To be clear, the people who point their fingers at a world in need, and call out the change agent as a "bleed-ing heart," are ultimately, suffering themselves. Deep down they yearn for connection, truth, and understanding. However, they are unable to go beyond their selfish and insular focus on ego and pride to see that they can be their own best solution to leading a richer and more meaningful existence. They do not have to be one of the soft-hearted people they so dislike. But if they can simply put their wall down for just a moment to let the light of others shine in, perhaps they too would recognize that there is a light that shines brightly within them, longing to be a beacon of hope and forgiveness.

The world is chock-full of circular conversations from people who use flawed, narcissistic logic and deception to advance the betterment of their personal life. The ego-driven mind is excellent at protecting our true selves and providing us with certainty and security. But we are at our best, including our having a chance of real security and being loved, when we go beyond our selfish wants and needs. Our intuition is a higher intelligence that resides within all humans and is connected to all living things. When our minds are shaped only by our unspiritual environments we tend to have a worldview that is limiting. When we open our minds to a higher consciousness, we can enter into the safety and security of a higher intelligence that guides us by our true intuition. It takes guts to make this connection, but it means ultimately knowing that the heart is what matters most.

MATTERS OF THE HEART: HOW TO SUPPORT COGNITIVE GROWTH AND TRANSFER EMOTIONAL WEALTH IN OUR KIDS

We are living in a fast-paced and ever-changing world. Rapid advancements in technology continually transform how we, learn, live our lives, and relate to each other. The swift and constant buzz of new and cool technical innovations has positive and negative implications on our daily lives. It also directly influences our children who are growing up, some might say, more quickly than ever.

Our kids are growing up with similar but also different kinds of challenges than we or our parents had. In many ways, we cannot fully appreciate or understand the scale or severity of the issues our kids face today. For example, our favorite pastime might have been playing an Atari, or better yet, stretching the phone cord out as far as we could to go around the corner into the adjacent room, just so we could to have a private call with a friend.

Kids today are cranking away on an Xbox or other gaming console with more computing capability than most regional banks had in 1990. They are also texting their friends at lightning speeds from their own blinged-out smartphone that features enhanced encryption and a fingerprint reader for additional security.

Think about it; young people's heroes in the 80s and 90s were musicians and athletes. What boy didn't wanna be "like Mike?" I'm pretty sure my older sister sprayed her bangs to new heights, not to call in a flock of seagulls (that might have happened once), but because the Madonna phase of development had kicked into adolescent overdrive. Kids today get bored with "common" celebrity. Dunking a basketball from the foul line takes extreme athleticism and is pretty cool to see once or twice. To become a gamer turned sensational YouTuber (yup, I'm talking about you DanTDM) . . . well, now you have your kids full-on attention.

If left alone, literally to their own (mobile) devices, children would have unabridged access to the unfiltered and unregulated content of the world, at least through the lens of YouTube, Google, Facebook, Instagram, texting, and other digital "screen time" services. At face value, one could argue that it is useful for children to see the world for what it is. But without appropriate contextual meaning and interpretation, it is more likely that a child could, just as an adult might, misinterpret fact from fiction and truth from reality. Furthermore, it's critical to take into consideration the cognitive and emotional implications of "screen time."

In four decades the economics and demographics of families and households have in shifted dramatically in the United States. Couple that with the fact that technology has infiltrated our communities, schools, and homes, presenting social and interpersonal dynamics and communications that we have yet to fully grasp or understand.

Let's face it, the days of whining about how we "walked to school up hill, both ways" are long over. Kids today are faced with a host of issues ranging from cyberbullying to mass desensitization of social issues, which far exceed the discomfort of a long walk home from school. The brave new world of 24/7 communications and media competes for everyone's attention. It also has real impacts on our children and family dynamics.

According to the American Heart Association (AHA) kids aged 8-to-18 spend on average seven hours a day looking at screens.[41] Nearly one-third of their life is spent in front of a screen, watching videos, engaging in social media, gaming, texting, and other forms of digital engagement and entertainment.

Studies has shown that excessive screen time can lead to significant health effects and learning disabilities including mood and personality changes, attention problems, obesity, sleep disruption, poor posture, and changes in social behaviors.

With this in mind, some useful suggestions to support home-healthy technology use and behaviors include:

- *Set them up for success.* Create opportunities for your kids to put good practices into place on how they use mobile devices. Establish restrictions (and set the device parameters) so that they cannot access any content or sites you deem inappropriate. Set them up for success with reasonable expectations, terms, incentives, and consequences. Let them see what successful and healthy digital behaviors looks like, not just the repercussions of non-conformance.

- *Let them know they can be boss.* Set limits on screen time. Help your kids understand that mobile devices do not manage their time; instead, they are the steward of the device.

- *Make it fun and get personal.* Use screen time in a purposeful way such as a learning aid or illustrative tool tied to homework or for supporting more family-focused time together. If going on a family road-trip, let them learn about GPS, maps, geography, and so on. Tie the experience into something they can do, like writing to a friend about their experience using key facts and new knowledge.

- *Model expected behavior.* Practice your own screen-time restraint by putting your phone away when your kids spend time with you. Put your phone away at least an hour before bedtime.

• ***Provide a moral compass and foundation.*** Outside of a very small "let's get started" index card; most digital technologies do not provide any guidelines for how they should be properly used and not misused. In that way, they are not smart, but dumb devices. The "conscious" side of technology comes from those that operate the device. Let kids engage, when appropriate, with technology so that they see their devices and apps for what they are: awesome tools and aids that help us communicate and experience life in enriched ways and not something to be abused or used in manipulative ways. Have frank discussion with them about what is right and wrong in digital communications. Remember it is not just about what they access, create or send— but also what is received from others. Their ability to communicate what's right and wrong within their peer group is critical to healthy behaviors.

Our children's immersion with technology is deeper and more influential than when we first played around with a calculator, digital television, or a first generation Nintendo game. We cannot sit by idle as external forces shape our children's personalities as they affect their self-respect or identity. Rather, we need to be giving our children time and attention, in meaningful ways, to build their character and spirit.

If it matters to you, it will matter to them. We have the opportunity to encourage our children to be self-aware, mindful, grateful, respectful, and caring. In a world besieged by deceptive tactics, divisive politics and derogatory demeanor, it is up to us, as parents (and citizens) to change this course.

We need to lead by example in all that we do. As we take the time to observe, play, and interact with our kids we can better understand how they are internalizing the world around them, and we can be there to support the healthy growth of their cognitive and emotional development.

PART THREE

★ ★ ★

The Role of Dignity in an Irrational World

The majority of time in my career has been designated to the craft of bringing stakeholders together to discuss and create mutual solutions. I like to think of this as "creating the island." When you are on a small island, you have limited resources, either what is native to the island or what you have taken with you to the island. Occasionally some extraneous item might wash ashore that can provide a use.

For the most part, you make the most of what is already on your small island for daily survival. The island is like the foundation of a partnership among two or several people. The island has some relatively fixed features such as location/geography, climate/topography, biome/ecosystem, natural resources, and risks/hazards. Given its array of "assets," I always begin with the question: Does this island have the basic and core requirements for it to be occupied by partners in a mutual way from the onset? Can the partners see the potential to survive?

Beyond that, do the partners see the opportunity to thrive together? If the partners choose to occupy this island together, how can they collaborate to construct a common vision of the island? In what ways do partners collaborate to toward creating a common culture and governance system for how they use natural resources? If there were to be any unintended damages, how can the partnership work to protect, enhance, and restore the island?

Island relationships are one metaphor for explaining the nuances of partnerships. Like people who must live together on a small island, partnerships represent the union of two or more unsuspecting parties who come together to cocreate toward a common objective. The art of partnership formation is not only about discovering we have in common; it's also about celebrating what makes us different and realizing that it is through our distinctions that we create purpose and value.

7

The Art of Possibility in a World of Constrained Resources

The basic tenet of life is survival. At its most raw composition, human survival means having the necessary food, shelter, and clothing to sustain life. The world's population now exceeds 7.6 billion people. If we view the principle of dignity from the context of our global population and our ability to provide a foundation for basic survivability, humans are drastically underperforming.

According to data and information gathered by Worldhunger. org[42] and DoSomething.org:[43,44]

- *Poor* – Nearly ½ of the world's population—more than 3 billion people—live on less than $2.50 a day. More than 1.3 billion live in extreme poverty—less than $1.25 a day. 80 percent of the world population lives on less than $10 a day.

- *Starving and Malnourished* – 815 million people worldwide do not have enough food to eat. Globally, 150 million children under the age five were stunted (reduced rate of growth and development) due to chronic malnutrition.

- *Lack Resources and Health Care* – More than 750 million people lack adequate access to clean drinking water. Diarrhea caused by inadequate drinking water, sanitation, and hand hygiene kills an estimated 842,000 people every year globally, or approximately 2,300 people per day. As of 2013, 21.8 million children under one year of age worldwide had not received the three recommended doses of vaccine against diphtheria, tetanus and pertussis. ¼ of all humans live without electricity—approximately 1.6 billion people.

- *Premature Deaths* – One billion children worldwide are living in poverty and 22,000 children die each day due to poverty. Preventable diseases like diarrhea and pneumonia take the lives of two million children a year who are too poor to afford proper treatment.

There have been financial estimates that it would require $30 billion to $100 billion to fully eradicate global hunger. Whether it is the lower or higher end of the range that is a lot of money. However, when you consider the fact that in 2018, US pet owners spent more than $72 billion on pet food alone, or that United States taxpayers foot the bill for more than $60 billion in health-care fraud each year, it does not seem unreasonable to financially address global hunger.[45]

From another perspective, if the ten wealthiest people on the planet chose to contribute 5 percent of their wealth toward addressing hunger that would equate to more than $30 billion. To be fair, most of the top ten wealthiest are already contributing larger portions of their wealth to foster greater dignity throughout the world. Whether their focus is on hunger, climate change, medical discoveries, technology, social leadership, or education, these billionaires are putting portions of their financial wealth to a higher use.

We can agree or disagree what cause these leaders direct their resources to. But seeding a society of good goes far beyond how much value is on a check. Money is an essential element for addressing complex and interrelated social, economic, and environmental challenge—but it is not the exclusive mechanism for creating change.

I am absolutely convinced that no wealth in the world can help humanity forward, even in the hands of the most devoted worker in this cause. The example of great and pure character is the only thing that can lead us to noble thoughts and deeds. Money only appeals to selfishness and irresistibly invites abuse. Can anyone imagine Moses, Jesus, or Gandhi armed with the money-bags of Carnegie?

—ALBERT EINSTEIN,
"The World As I See It," 1934

The World's Billionaires, 2019					
No.	Name	Nationality	Net Worth	Age	Source(s) of Wealth
1	Jeff Bezos	United States	$111.6 billion	55	Amazon
2	Bill Gates	United States	$106.5 billion	64	Microsoft
3	Bernard Arnault	France	$104.1 billion	70	LVMH
4	Warren Buffett	United States	$85 billion	89	Berkshire Hathaway
5	Mark Zuckerberg	United States	$71.8 billion	35	Facebook
6	Amancio Ortega	Spain	$70.3 billion	83	Zara
7	Larry Ellison	United States	$67.4 billion	75	Oracle
8	Carlos Slim	Mexico	$61.9 billion	79	América Móvil
9	Larry Page	United States	$58.1 billion	46	Google
10	Françoise Bettencourt Meyers	France	$53.2 billion	66	L'Oréal

SOURCE: The World's Billionaires, Wikipedia

It's interesting to point out that as of 2019 there is now one woman represented on the top 10 world's billionaire's list, Françoise Bettencourt Meyers, the only daughter and heiress of Liliane Bettencourt, the family who owns the company L'Oréal. Interestingly, she is also an author of Bible commentaries and works on Jewish-Christian relations. Also note that 6 out of 10 represent a United States nationality. Two years prior, 8 out of 10 of the billionaires on the list represented US nationality. Further note that the average age of the top 10 wealthiest is 66 years old (including Mark Zuckerberg whose ripe young age of 35 brings the average age of this billionaire list down a few years). It's reasonable to predict that in the next two decades this list will change dramatically. It will likely shift to be more diverse including more women, a younger average age, and more representation from other nations.

There is something about getting older that translates into giving back. It's not just having the financial means to be philanthropic, it's a maturity and understanding of what one deems virtuous and important to them. I cannot speak for any of these philanthropic leaders, but I know what I thought about in my 20s and 30s was much different than what I know put my mind to thinking about in my 40s. This is not so say the capacity for giving becomes greater as one ages versus when they are younger. People tend to give more financially when they have the means to do so, and often that correlates to the accumulation of vast financial wealth over a sustained period of time, often decades.

I point this out in part to make a point. The single greatest opportunity you, me and we have right now, today, is to not wait one, two, three or more decades until we feel like we have the financial freedom to "do something good." That is a fallacy that holds us as individuals and as a society back from being great. While the financial wealth accumulation of billionaires is awesome, it is also an extreme measure that 99 percent of the people on Earth will ever attain.

Solving the world's problems should not be [exclusively] about pointing the finger at the 1 percent and asking, "look what you did . . . what can you do for me?" Rather, it should be more about the 99 percent asking, "how can we, with strength in numbers and conviction, attain a better life together, as a unified team?" This is not intended to be altruistic and circular logic on the fundamentals of the global economy, democracy or the ascension of wealth in "rigged" economies.

We have the power, knowledge, intellect, and capacity to be and do great things right here and now. We do not have to wait for permission or for the bank account to amass a fortune. We simply have to surrender our pride and ego to the idea that society thrives when individuals thrive. For individuals to thrive we all need to serve and play and integral role in living and leading a dignified existence.

- Global change that affects our life and the life of our children are happening now! We need to respect and embrace that fact.

- Through individual decisions and behaviors (Accountability), you have control over your life and can influence the life of others and the world around you. By choosing to take action as far as your individual accountability, you choose to engage in a life of purpose and consequence for today and the future.

- Deferring decisions to take action can increase probabilities for negative consequences in our future.

- Living a lifestyle just to keep the status-quo negates the possibility of sustainability. To work for sustainability means continually looking at your life and asking, "What can I do to improve this condition? And the condition of those around me?"

Technological and product solutions exist to create a more just and sustainable world. Today, we have the knowledge and innovation to make incredible advancements in how we conserve and consume natural resources, energy, and water. The question is, do we have the political will, personal temperament, and focused leadership to put solutions in place for the betterment of all of humanity, not just for bettering the lives of a few?

Achieving sustainability requires more than vision. It requires an incredible amount of teamwork, collaboration, and contribution. By thinking of a shared future and establishing concrete "Attainability" targets, organizations (and society) have a clearer path to achieve their sustainability goals.

Dignity in Business: The Next Wave Will Be Human-Centered Value Creation

I could not write this book without reflecting upon entrepreneurship and business. My career has been spent in discovering dignity in business and life. That is, how can individuals and businesses wield their influence in ways that protect, enhance, value, and celebrate diversity of life and all of its forms?

The environmental context of business has always been near and dear to me. Since I was a young child, I have been interested in and concerned with ecosystem protection and conservation. I grew up in the heart of the Finger Lakes region of New York State, surrounded by the beauty and wonder of natural resources. During my youth, I spent time exploring the natural environment around me. I fished the lakes with my dad, got muddy in streams and ponds with friends as we looked for frogs, and built forts under the canopy of woodlands. Through it all, I learned to appreciate and have respect for life in all of its brilliant forms.

When business sustainability became popularized in the late 1990s and early 2000s, I was enthralled. The idea that business products, processes, and operations can be designed at the onset or reengineered in place to protect, enhance, or restore environmental quality intrigued me.

As a result, I invested my undergraduate and graduate education into learning and discovering how people and the planet could coexist. I immersed myself in researching and understanding how innovative start-up as well as mature multinational corporations operate.

Fast forward two decades and the business sustainability has become more prominent, particularly as the business of sustainability has taken root and created a generation of thought leaders, change agents, and practitioners who, like me, share a purpose of shaping how business can be a force for good.

Today there are many forces shaping the context of business including, The Paris Agreement, the UN's Sustainable Development Goals (SDGs), the evolution of B Corporations, and the continued proliferation of corporate-defined business practices within frameworks such as corporate social responsibility (CSR), corporate sustainability, and "net positive" restorative businesses. For example:

- The Paris Agreement attempts to evoke a concerted global response to ward of the threat of climate change. The agreement seeks to keep the global temperature rise below 2 degrees Celsius (above pre-industrial levels). To achieve this, the agreement established a framework for building the necessary financial, technology, and geo-political-business capacity building frameworks in place. The agreement entered into force on November 4, 2016, a date when 55 parties to the convention had agree to the Agreement.[46]

- The United Nations (UN) Sustainable Development Goals (SDGs),[47] a collection of 17 global goals, were established to address social and economic development issues. In September 2015 the UN convened in New York and put into place, a declaration[48] for sustainable development which outlined the 17 SDGs. The SDGs are based on the UN's framework for enacting a plan of action for people, planet, prosperity, peace, and partnership. To this end the UN seeks to strengthen "universal peace in larger freedom." One of the central tenets of the UN's agenda is eradicating poverty in all of its forms including hunger and disease. Further, the UN's SDGs also focus in on "universal respect for human rights and human dignity, the rule of law, justice, equality and non-discrimination; of respect for race, ethnicity and cultural diversity; and of equal opportunity permitting the full realization of human potential and contributing to shared prosperity."

- B-Corporations (B Corps) are "for-profit companies certified by the nonprofit B Lab to meet rigorous standards for social and environmental performance, accountability, and transparency. The B Corp community is rapidly growing. As of 2018 there are more than 2,500 B Corps from more than 50 countries representing more than 130 industries. The B Corp community "envisions a global economy that uses business as a force for good." B Corps are purpose-driven businesses that "create benefits for all stakeholders, not just shareholders."

- The B Corp "Declaration of Interdependence"[49] further states: *As B Corporation and Leaders of this emerging economy, we believe: That we must be the change we seek in the world. That all business ought to be conducted as if people and place mattered. That, through their products, practices, and profits, businesses should aspire to do no harm and benefit all. To do so requires that we act with the understanding that we are each dependent upon another and thus responsible for each other and future generations.*

- Restorative Businesses are companies that proactively choose to design environmental restoration into their products, services and operations. These companies pursue sustainable impact with a strong sense of purpose and typically go way above and beyond regulatory compliance and their social license to operate. Restorative companies do not believe in waste. Instead, restorative companies look at everything as a resource which can be optimized and used more efficiently and productively for the benefit of the enterprise. As a result, restorative companies dramatically account for and reduce their impact on natural resources; and further, they have a net positive environmental return. Companies including Fetzer Vineyards and HARBEC, Inc. have successfully embraced ecologic restoration into their business culture, strategy and operations yielding net positive gains on the triple bottom line (people, profit, planet). The case studies on Fetzer Vineyards and HARBEC embellish upon the power of restorative business strategies.

It is awesome to see how geopolitical and business forces are working together to create a more just, peaceful, and sustainable world. The Paris Agreement, UN SDGs, and advent of B Corps and restorative business strategies each illustrate examples of dignity in business at work. While many would argue that business has a long way to go toward delivering dignity at scale, it is important to reflect on just how far business has come and to celebrate those organizations choosing to lead a more dignified existence. It is also prudent to recognize that businesses are not impenetrable, unreachable, or ambiguous organisms. Businesses are accessible living things that are comprised of people. People have hearts and are the beating heart of any organization. As such, businesses can, just as people can, be transformed to serve as a force for good.

Dignity in business is attained when all stakeholders of the business have a voice that is heard and listened to and enveloped into the culture, strategy, operating system, and measured impact and performance of the enterprise's people, processes, and profits. Dignity in business then, is the underlying code of conduct by which its purpose is defined and put into action. Dignity for business is a license to operate, a fundamental right to serve and be in business in the first place. If business fails to live up to its dignity code, customers, shareholders, and stakeholders will react and push back on its very foundation resulting in either a correction in behavior or complete cease of operations.

A Double Shot of Indignity: Facing Implicit and Blatant Racial Bias

In April 2018, a Starbucks manager at a Philadelphia, Pennsylvania, location called police on two African American men who were waiting for a friend at the retail establishment. As the story goes, the two men were quietly waiting for a friend but had not purchased anything at the store. One of the men asked to use the restroom and was denied because he was not a paying customer. The location manager called the police who arrived and arrested the two men for trespassing but later let them go without charges. The event stirred a great deal of emotion and drew into question the prevalence of racial bias at the world's leading coffee brand. The incident resulted in Starbucks issuing numerous apologies and instituting classes in rooting out racial bias. On May 29, 2018, Starbucks closed 8,000 of its retail stores in North America to conduct anti-bias training for its employees.

The training, which included approximately 175,000 Starbucks store employees as well as its headquarters focused on "understanding prejudice and the history of public accommodations in the United States."[50] The training was received with mixed responses. According to some reports, employees felt uncomfortable by the training while others noted that it was productive and enlightening.[51] Some of Starbucks baristas who participated in the training felt that it was "wishy-washy" and lacked substance on how it could be implemented in real-world situations. The curriculum of the training also was criticized for perpetuating racial stigmas, potentially inflicting more harm than good,[52] based upon one of its core messages, which challenged individuals to become more "color brave" in their daily life.

Society and business are both losing ground, however. We are allowing self-doubt to override self-respect as we push deeper and deeper into a society quick to blame and slow to forgive. It is no wonder more and more people point their finger at Big Business and Big Government for challenges they faced.

Health care, energy prices, pollution, wage disparity, poverty, hunger, disease, natural resource depletion and degradation, water scarcity and climate change—these are just a sample of the issues that persist today, all in need of our full attention and pragmatic solutions.

Although there is significant evidence about how Big Business and Big Government have magnified and perpetuated unsustainable business models, assigning blame will get us nowhere. The truth is we need to point our finger to ourselves and ask what role we have played in this equation. What role can we play to move beyond blaming people and organizations and toward a more sustainable future?

Our reality is that we all represent citizens and consumers, but we are also parents, teachers, community activists, policy makers, designers, and business and government leaders. We do not clock-in and clock-out of life by putting on a different hat to wear to our jobs. When I talk about sustainability, I am talking about a philosophy, a mindset, and a discipline—like leadership—which needs to be enveloped in all that we are, and all that we do, for it to have an impact on our state of affairs.

Sustainability also has to be put into effect. It is not enough to think about ideals. We have to put them into practice if they are to have any value, consequence, or impact. Thus sustainability needs to be exercised each day if it has any chance of achieving a level of strength and flexibility that is high performing.

In the past, there have been two major actors addressing economic and policy considerations for sustainability: business and government. They supported society, balanced each other, and enabled, at least in the United States, generations of improved growth, and progress. Today, social actors are influencing our collective mindset more rapidly and with greater conviction than business or government. Social media, for instance, has proven itself to be a tremendous factor for mobilizing people around issues quickly. The art of storytelling and act of owning the narrative have proven to be effective means of motivating people and stimulating social change.

Our definition of progress is changing. Today we don't only value currency and trade as indicators of success. We also value the right to exercise our human right to protect our health from being endangered by the environment and consider the right to vote for universal healthcare an element of a democracy. In the past century, a great deal of emphasis was placed on economic progress, often at the detriment of human health and the environment. Today we continue to clean up our pollution of the past while working to limit waste from our more modern processes. We are not perfect, but slowly moving in the right direction.

As a concept and discipline, the word "sustainability" is like "leadership." It is hard to define, there are varied points of view about it, and we all know it is in short supply and needed more than ever.

In the late 60s, environmental movement was born out of necessity, in order to change the laws on pollution and waste.

Today we have the intellect to foresee environmental risk and have a mindset of prevention about what we do about it, but how can we alleviate human-induced risks from occurring in the first place?

Sustainability is more than the pursuit of "green" or an exclusive focus on the environment. While sustainability's roots run deep in environmental awareness, there are other elements including the economy, social needs, international affairs, public policy, education, health care, and national security that are also essential as part of the discussion:

- Taking action on sustainability through personal accountability: Improving your life context can happen by being open-minded and allowing sustainability to open a doorway to a better you. Here are some perspectives to consider:

  Assess and understand your "life context," that is, how you are currently living your life

  Define what having sustainability can mean to your life

  Simplify sustainability to suit your lifestyle

  Be accountable to you and those around you

  Take action on sustainability and improving your life in the context of being sustainable

  Share your successes of contributing to sustainability

  Make room for spirituality

- How do we move society toward living and attaining sustainability versus aspiring to change? How do we become doers, not just bystanders or thinkers? We need to mobilize our generation to take action, not just fall victim to personal complacency and tolerance of the status-quo.

- Achieving sustainability requires more than vision. It requires an incredible amount of deliberate teamwork, collaboration, and contribution. By thinking of a shared future and establishing concrete "Attainability" targets, organizations (and society) have a clearer path to achieve their sustainability goals. Technological and product solutions exist, *but there is no silver bullet!* We have the knowledge and innovation to make incredible advancements in how we conserve and consume natural resources, energy, and water. We cannot [exclusively] buy our way to a "greener, sustainable, better, holistic, peaceful, and just "eco" future.

  Industry has models for restorative products (and companies) that are working to achieve a mutual contract between planet, people, and prosperity.

- Do we have the personal, political, and generational will to (1) accept that change is imminent and (2) take swift action to address this change?

- Sustainability is the core of life itself. To sustain life we need to be interdependent on each other and upon how "you, me, and we" can take personal and collective responsibility for our behaviors, as citizens and consumers.

Sustainability relies on our ability to integrate the past, the present, and the future. We have to account for prior knowledge, and we have to make hard but smart decisions in the present. We also cannot forget that our future is partly unknown and partly defined by our own hands and doing. Ultimately, the foundation and formula for a sustainable world (in our community, economy, and business) is grounded by people and our treatment of each other. The question is, do we have the will to act and the ability to sustain proactive action over time?

Carrying Dignity Across Generational Divides: A Dreamer Who Dares to Dance

Mr. Fernando Paiz and La Ruta Maya Foundation[53]

Fernando Paiz, President of La Ruta Maya Foundation and upcoming museum, is the quintessential Renaissance man. He is a philanthropist, businessman, cultural and environmental preservationist, humanitarian, father and grandfather. His storied life has yielded many titles and credits to his name.

A serial entrepreneur, Paiz is the founder and builder of progressive businesses, and was the first to introduce Internet and Cable TV services in Guatemala and the first to introduce PET bottles in South America. He also oversees several agricultural, energy, hospitality, and real-estate developments in Guatemala, Nicaragua, El Salvador, and Honduras.

Do you enjoy frozen mangos in your fruit smoothies? You can thank, in part, Fernando Paiz who invested in the cultivation of mangos for local consumption and as an export product to the United States. Fueled by a strong work ethic and a desire to help others, Paiz's business interests are far reaching. In 2012 with the help of his capital, Nicaragua's first frozen foods facility was established to process tons of mango cubes per year. Paiz is an active owner and developer of multi-megawatt solar energy installations in Honduras and a geothermal plant in Nicaragua and is also a key strategy partner in sustainable real-estate developments, like Itz'ana Resorts & Residences and Ka'ana Resort in Belize.

Paiz demonstrated an ability to solve problems at an early age working at his family's business, La Fragua, a retail company that his father founded more than 80 years ago. In 2005, the shareholders in the company decided to bring in a strategic investor, Walmart. The partnership proved successful. This investment resulted the first time Walmart had a presence in Central America's retail marketplace and eventually culminated in the sale of the company to Walmart Mexico a few years later.

While Paiz has had great success in business, one of his most personal and treasured endeavors continues to unfold. Recently, I caught up with him to learn more about La Ruta Maya Conservation Foundation, and his unwavering commitment to protect and preserve the rich Maya heritage in the region.

The La Ruta Maya Conservation Foundation is a private organization dedicated to rescuing and preserving pre-Columbian art and antiquities, in many cases receiving donations of them abroad so that the pieces are returned to Guatemala for legal registration and offered for exhibitions in his country's museums. The La Ruta Maya Foundation seeks to enrich public education, national pride, and the celebration of the Maya and Mesoamerican cultures.

La Ruta Maya Foundation was established in 1990 by Wilbur Garrett, then editor of National Geographic Magazine. Since then, the foundation has registered more than 3,000 archaeological artifacts which have been carefully restored, conserved, and presently made accessible to researchers and the public.

Fernando Paiz's interest in Maya artifacts was stimulated when he was a 10-year-old boy looking for broken shards of ancient pottery with a childhood friend at a construction site on Roosevelt Boulevard that exits the city of Guatemala. "It's very unfortunate." Paiz noted. "Highways and buildings were built on top of many significant archeological sites, as was the case of pre-classic Kaminal Juyú (300 BCE), a most important city in antiquity in the valley of Guatemala. In the past there has been looting of Maya sites and illegal trading and export of important pieces. In an effort to stop this, today we have regulations and enforcement in place to deter the theft and deliberate destruction of Maya sites."

It was later in life that Paiz discovered his passion for preserving Maya antiquities. He recalled the specific moment: "I was working for my father in our family store. I was 15 years old then. A gentleman came into the office and asked my father to buy a plate from him. My father had no interest, so the man asked me if I wanted to buy it. I looked at this colorful piece depicting what appeared to be a ceremonial dance. I loved it immediately and bought the piece for the equivalent of $1. That was a lot of money in those days, especially for me as my salary was quite modest. But I loved the beauty of the piece and wanted to ensure it remained protected."

It was this plate that would continue to inspire him and serve as the backdrop to his life-long dream and journey to return and restore historic artifacts so that the significance of the Maya culture can enrich the lives of this and future generations.

Paiz recalled that while he saw the plate as beautiful, it was his high school history teacher that explained the significance and age of the plate. "I discovered the power of storytelling captured in the art and imagery of the pottery and immediately felt the responsibility for being a caretaker of this one small window to the past."

The Mesoamerican cultural area spans from southern Mexico into Central America. Recognized as one of the six fundamental "cradles of civilization," Maya culture spawned some of the most complex agricultural societies and cities, art and architecture, advanced mathematics astronomy and writing systems—and widely known for their remarkably complex calendars dating back to the 5th century BCE.

He added, "The Maya were a sophisticated society. They developed advanced urbanism in their cities with complex engineering for water management. Their knowledge of mathematics, astronomy, and fully developed writing system with formal grammatical rules and language allowed them to develop major buildings and one of the most accurate calendars in existence. To celebrate Maya culture through the preservation and protection of their history and heritage is a celebration of humanity and life itself."

With financial support from Fernando Paiz, the La Ruta Maya Foundation is working to put context to each of the more than 3,000 pieces in its collection. The Foundation has received grants from the Smithsonian Institute and other organizations and sponsors in an effort to test the clay of unique pieces of their collection. Using scientific methods and processes including thermo luminescence (TL) and atomic testing to identify the place and date the pieces were made, the Foundation seeks to understand more about who, how, why, and when select artifacts were created and used. By incorporating sound science into their stewardship of Maya antiquities, the Foundation is advancing our knowledge of how Maya people communicated, worked, and lived.

Having public accessibility to these objects, are also pillars of preserving antiquities. Paiz remarked, "Sustaining Maya culture happens not only through the preservation of material objects . . . the culture truly lives on when we can share and expand upon the richness of Maya culture through first-hand experience, interpretation, awareness, and education. In an effort to extend our reach beyond Central America, we are sharing unique pieces from La Ruta Maya Foundation's collection for exhibition at other museums around the world."

Showcasing La Ruta Maya Foundation's important collection of pre-Columbian artifacts has been a deliberate strategy to raise global awareness of Guatemala's cultural heritage and a means of demonstrating national pride.

Mr. Paiz is building support to establish Museo Maya de America as a place where science, education, research, cultural and economic interests can come together. The proposed Museo Maya de America would house the National Museum of Archeology and Ethnography of Guatemala, together with visiting exhibits and private collections. This would anchor traditional ethnology yet also bridge cultural heritage and patrimony in ways that connect the past in meaningful ways of understanding our generation.

Mr. Paiz dreams of the day when Maya collections can be exhibited, side-by-side, with visiting collections from cradles of civilization like Egypt, the Indus Valley, and China. "Can you imagine," Paiz said, "artifacts from early Egyptian civilization on display right next to Maya? What an incredible opportunity for comparative assessment, discovery and learning about the origins of humanity."

In 2014 it was announced that the building of the Museo Maya de América was to be designed by the Boston-based architectural firm Harry Gugger Studio with Seis Arquitectos architecture firm in Guatemala in collaboration with over, under. The building design is inspired by the distinctive art and architectural features of Maya civilization. Mr. Paiz provided seed funding for the design of the facility and actively worked with regional and global partners toward the launch of a $100 million fundraising campaign.

Paiz's vision is for the Museo Maya de America to be an inclusive center of knowledge for scientists, researchers, students, tourists, and cultural enthusiasts alike. The project could be a boon for Guatemala's economy and global reputation as a destination which converges art, culture, and history with contemporary infrastructure and amenities.

He believes the completed project will increase visits to Guatemala City, and tourism could yield more than one percent to Guatemala's annual gross domestic product.

The Levón Institute at the University of Vaasa conducted an economic impact study of museums and found that they contribute significantly to the regional service economy including transportation, accommodations, food and beverage, and entertainment. As noted in the Levón Institute study, museum's activities also contribute to education/academic and research investments tied to universities, foundations, government organizations, and other regional businesses.

Our generation has a historic challenge and opportunity before it. The life we choose to lead today has a lasting impact and impression on tomorrow. Sustainability is about having clarity of mind and presence. It's also about treasuring the life we have and celebrating life in and for the moment. Sustainability is much like a dance, fluid and flowing, with one foot rooted in the past and the other directing the future. The mechanics of our dance can be beautiful, but when we are out of rhythm with the beat of the earth and stars, we ungracefully stumble.

It's nice to know that people like Fernando Paiz exist, thirsting for knowledge, eager to give, and unafraid to dance. Preserving the past, protecting the present, and promising a better future—that's where passion and purpose collide for Mr. Paiz and his dream to establish the Museo Maya de America for Guatemala City and the world.

8

The Meaning of True Dignity

Don't Join the Doomed Zombie Apocalypse

There is a light that shines in almost all of us. Let your light shine brightly to be a beacon of hope and humility, particularly in our world that is struggling to illuminate a path free of fear and hopelessness. I know this to be true: You shine the brightest, and are serving yourself and humanity the best, when you are being true to yourself.

Humanity is under assault. Although aliens seeking to destroy all of humanity on Independence Day have yet to attack us, one could argue that we are falling victim to a universal zombie apocalypse. Let me explain.

Each day people fight for their survival. The poorest of poor, the wealthiest one percent, and those somewhere in between all are living to live another day. As most people understand, financial wealth is no indicator of a person's self-worth, integrity, or dignity. Financial wealth may keep you living comfortably, but it has not yet proven to be a force to keep any of us from aging or dying.

We place too much emphasis on financial wealth in our society. Happiness, success, love, kindness, gratitude, and a host of other emotions and successful outcomes from our goals outcomes can be attained without great financial wealth. Yet day after day, year after year, a large majority of people dedicate their time to the pursuit of more money, more things, more for the sake of more. Too often people come on the backside of achieving financial success and attaining more stuff only to feel as empty as a water well in a desert. What they thirst for is not material or monetary; it is something much more visceral and accessible.

We all share a common humanity, but not all of us tap into our intellect, spirituality, and consciousness in the same way or at the same time. Thus, while humans have great capacity for love and mutual respect, at any given time the humanity of our society is modulating up and down like waves in the ocean. We rise and fall as individuals and as a society at the hands of our own doing.

Therefore, thinking you might be living in a zombie apocalypse looks something like this:

- If you see people going through life with perfect eyesight but blind to what is happening in the world around them, well, they might be a zombie.

- If you see people going through life with perfect hearing but unable to listen without passing judgment or criticism to others . . . well, they might just be a zombie.

- If people want to text or direct message you as the only means of communication, well, they might as well be a zombie.

- If you find yourself devoid of any tangible (nondigital) connection with another human being, be it touch, conversation, having a bite to eat, laughing hysterically, playing sports, going for a walk, or even just sitting quietly together, well, then you might be a zombie in the making.

- If you find that you or anyone has become numb, indifferent, or apathetic to horrific events in your community or around the world, then the process of zombification is well underway, and I suggest you break free from the person before it is too late.

I hope you will not join the zombie apocalypse. It is downright frightening. As much good technology has enriched our lives with, it also has its limitations and challenges. Sure, technology enables us to constantly be in the know and connected. That is great, right? Well, no offense to the millions of people who post and like videos of cats dressed up as prominent historical figures, honestly, I do not feel I want to know you. What you and your pets do in the sanctuary of your home is completely up to you, but having fun posting this while making your pets uncomfortable instead of doing something more worthwhile seems ridiculous.

The zombification of humans has made us ambivalent, numb, and overwhelmed. Society has shifted, culturally and practically, to a disturbing place where we no longer have to keep honest dialog with one another (let alone ourselves). In fact, distrust is now so entrenched that the merits of a free, just, and open society are being challenged daily. For example, research by the global communication and marketing firm Edelman[54] suggests that the majority of the viewing public has become highly skeptical and cynical about the integrity and focus of mainstream news organizations.

Edelman is one of the preeminent experts and sources of how trust is measured in society. Leveraging more than eighteen years of data and greater than 33,000 survey respondents, Edelman produces an annual *Trust Barometer Global Report* which provides critical insights into society's trust with key institutions including business, government, media, and nongovernment organizations (NGOs).

According to Edelman's *2018 Trust Barometer Global Report*, nearly seven out of ten people "worry about false information or fake news being used as a weapon" worldwide. Across the globe, and particularly in the United States, uncertainty over whether news is fake or real has magnified since the 2016 presidential election.

In their *2018 Report* Edelman also reported that 66 percent of people believe news organizations are "more concerned with attracting a big audience than reporting." They further reported that 65 percent of people believe news organizations "sacrifice accuracy to be the first to break a story"; hence our current media culture of streaming "Breaking News." And Edelman's research further noted that 59 percent of people believe that modern news organizations, once pillars of independent reporting to the public, now "support an ideology vs. informing the public."

Deep in our hearts, I believe we all come from a place of hope, goodness, honesty, and truth. When basic survival comes from a place of "me before them" versus "one for all and all for one," well, most people will typically default to the former and seek to protect themselves first.

Consider this example of a change in the business world. Years ago an open and honest conversation resulting in a business deal between two people might have been avowed with a handshake. As time when on, we put into place legal contacts facilitated by lawyers who worked as "honest brokers" to ensure each party met their intended obligations. If any party failed to meet their obligations, they could be sued by the other. In addition, years later we moved even further away from the conversation and handshake. "Human-independent" digital innovations like blockchain stand to create a more transparent, real-time, and trusted ledger of business dealings and decisions. Slowly but persistently across time, we have decided that we inherently do not trust other people, in life, love, or business. Thus, we have created entirely new professions, academic disciplines, technologies, processes, businesses, and infrastructures to protect us from each other.

This is not a gripe about technology or your choice on whether, how, when or why to interface with it. If you want to take videos of your dog windsurfing while wearing the latest in doggie fashions, by all means do it, especially if it brings joy to you and others. If you feel that buying your home leveraging new blockchain technology offers you greater security or peace of mind, use it.

This book's purpose is to illuminate the fact that "you, me, and we" are the common denominator to a more just, peaceful, and sustainable world. While we individually may not be able to have an impact on every person on Earth, we can, through our individual actions and behaviors, have a profound impact on what Rodney Bullard, author of the book *Heroes Wanted* defines as the "three feet in front of us." If each of us hold ourselves and each other to a higher code of conduct and morality we can attain a more dignified existence, together.

I have come to appreciate people in life who give their service to others from a place of love, respect, and selflessness. We need more people like that in the world and in our lives. Each of us has great capacity to love and to be loved. We need humanity to be more humane. We need a greater sense of dignity and purpose in the world. Nothing in life is free or granted. It has to be earned and attained. Life is and should be for every human being, brilliant and beautiful. We all have in our DNA an underlying biological code for survival. We also have a spiritual and emotional code for enlightened connection, love, and respect. We need to tap into, understand, and put to use, both codes to live a purpose-driven and enriched life. The convergence of our biological and spiritual elements represent our "dignity code." The dignity code embodies our individual and collective past, present and future. It is the construct which differentiates humankind.

Everyone wants to be treated with respect and fairly. To live the life of our dreams, we must be willing to give of ourselves, to work hard for what we believe in, and to project and command a code of dignity in all that we do. It should be no surprise that rooted deep in religion, philosophy, and spirituality there are frameworks that attempt to guide our moral code. Examples include:

The Golden Rule: Treat others how you want to be treated.
The Golden Rule from the Bible, in the insightful words of Georgia D. Lee,[55] "is a journey into the way you think of, feel about, and speak to others."

The Law of Attraction in the terms of "New Thought" is a mind-power paradigm and philosophy that believes that we can wield positive or negative experiences in our life by focusing our thoughts accordingly. The Law of Attraction postulates that people and their thoughts are comprised of "pure energy" which can attract "like" energies when it is manifested to do so. While the New Thought Law of Attraction has no scientific actuation and has many opponents as well as proponents, it has been popularized in modern culture by many books and films including *The Secret* and by well-known personalities, including the comedian, actor, and artist, Jim Carrey.[56]

The Norm of Reciprocity in several fields of the social science of psychology is set forth as an expectation that people will repay in-kind, what another person has done for us. The Norm of Reciprocity is thought of as a "powerful engine for motivating, creating, sustaining, and regulating the cooperative behavior required for self-sustaining social organizations, controlling the damage done by unscrupulous, and contributing to social system stability."[57]

The Golden Rule, Law of Attraction, and Norm of Reciprocity represent a sample of the social-psychological frameworks humans have devised to maintain a sense of peace, justice, and order in society. The constructs of religion, government, media, business, and other institutions are also, along with these frameworks, mechanisms by which humans have established doctrines and principles that work to protect and serve individuals and societies.

With thousands of years of history and experience behind us, humans continue to be philosophically challenged. The ethics, values and morality of every human on Earth is shared, yet also unique. Nobody wants to be told what they can or should believe in, just as nobody wants to be limited in their life or told what to do. Freedom to pursue your beliefs and convictions should be a right, but it also needs to be grounded so that the ideals of one never come exclusively at the burden or detriment of another. Our "dignity code" is visceral, it's what keeps us focused on a common morality and yet enables us to be individually unique.

Being human is physical, spiritual, emotional, biological, and metaphysical. To live the best life possible requires us to reach our fullest potential as a physical/biological, emotional, and spiritual beings. The material world we put so much credence in represents a small part of what we truly are about or come from. We are so much more than the house we dwell in, the car that we drive, or the watch that adorns our wrist and mocks us when we are running late. We are so much more than the numbers that measure our weight, represent our net worth, or remind us how many friends and likes we have on social media. We objectify life and portray a distorted version of success by simplistic numbers that measure little if anything about a person. Yet, day after day, week after week, and year after year we fixate on things like our weight, our retirement savings, or how many likes our newest post on Facebook just registered. These numbers do not account to a hill of beans. The character, integrity, kindness, joy, love and impact of a person is best measured by how they treat others as well as themselves. This measure of humanity has been devalued, distorted and perverted by a society that has grown distrustful and cynical about each other.

We are beyond the proverbial crossroads. Let's face it. Humans have taken the wrong path. Instead of living up to the full potential of our DNA codes we've only tapped a small fraction of our self-worth. That has resulted in generations of people continuing to accept negative behaviors we are exposed to and playing out the same behaviors, personas, and roles that continue to degrade other humans and society as a whole. Whether we realize it or not, many of us are active participants in the zombie apocalypse which plagues humanity's ability to achieve greater things. Each time we allow another human being to degrade us or others we become more zombie-like.

Now is the time for us to assess our situation logically and put into place a plan for getting us back on course. We must dig and claw our way back to a generation of believers, doers, innovators, idealists, and dreamers who lift themselves up while they help others climb out of the abyss. We need people to rediscover what it means to put their faith and trust in others, and, likewise, to have others put their faith and trust in them. The time to end suffering, hatred, violence, bigotry, and other forms of deliberate assault on humanity grounded in a lack of self-respect is now. If humanity has any chance at survival we must stop the zombie apocalypse from advancing any further than it already has. To get started we must willingly choose to identify and discuss the implicit biases we all have and retrain our minds to embrace more heart in all that we are and do.

The mass desensitization and zombification of humanity has to stop and it can stop with us. What do you stand for? Who are you at heart? What is your dignity code? Let others know who you are and what is important to you. Use the power of positive thinking and positive influence. We can be the agents for action, trust, accountability, self-worth, and respect for all of life.

We can passively watch the woes of the world unfold on our four-inch screens and choose to weigh-in only when it is convenient and comfortable to do so. Anyone reading this knows that it is not enough to tweet or write a book if we are going to have an impact, we must take action and be accountable to ourselves, our families and communities. To fight the zombie-like people in our midst, we have to do something fundamentally outrageous and creative—we must actually talk to them. When we fail to keep honest dialogs with people we ultimately fail ourselves.

Out of the Head, into the Heart

The incident I discussed at Syracuse University is not isolated or unique, but a reflection of what's (deplorably and unfortunately] been going on more broadly in our communities across the country for a long time. If ignored or left unaddressed, fear, hatred, and bigotry breed more of the same. One of the reasons racism, misogyny, xenophobia, or other prejudices continue to perpetuate, generation after generation, is that we haven't done a good enough job of proactive dialog and discourse about this to shift hearts and minds.

When racism occurs, for example, in a company or community and is treated exclusively through a lens of crisis management to minimize damage to our reputation, there is no opportunity for the underlying issue and root cause to be openly vetted. Nobody wants to have a public-relations nightmare. When we handle instances of hate or bigotry with kid gloves, we essentially tell society that we know this is happening, we've addressed what happened, but we're not willing to acknowledge or treat the longer-term malignancy because we're unwilling to recognize that a malignancy exists, or we're too afraid of what else we may find or what we cannot control.

Hate perpetuates itself because people grow up experiencing or being taught hatred. People do not come out of the womb as haters. Well, there may have been a couple over the course of history (Hitler comes to mind). People are influenced to hate or to develop bias based upon their environment, what they experience, who they engage with, and how they are personally treated. From the second we take our first breath, our life circumstance begins to get shaped by factors external to the mother who carried us in a cozy home for nine months. As external factors weigh in on our psyche, we inherently develop biases to our surroundings, including other people, from our mechanisms for survival.

What we can all do to stop the proliferation of hatred, violence, racism, and so forth is to become unrelenting stewards of dignity, hope, and kindness. Starting this very day, you can change the world, for yourself and anyone you meet, by simply being kind. Beyond that, we need to carry that conviction forward to each successive generation by teaching and guiding them to be stewards of dignity in their own right. Our number one job is to care for ourselves and care for others, with a sense of humility and kindness that will ultimately transform hearts and minds.

Universities, like broader society, are a melting pot of people with different backgrounds, races, religions, and experiences. Unlike broader society however, the composition of students, faculty and staff for most universities do not fully reflect the "real world."

To break the cycle of unconscious bias we need to be teachers. We must communicate, openly and freely, and listen without judgment to each other. We must empower ourselves and each other to rise-up, take a swift and firm stance against prejudice and hatred, wherever and whenever it rears its ugly head. We must live our individual and collective lives by a higher code and set of principles guided by a values-system and morality that is not limited by any one ideology but represented and elevated by the fact that we are all created equal, that we are all interrelated, and that almost all of us deserve to be treated with the utmost dignity and respect each day of our lives.

Death with Dignity

Death is an uncomfortable topic for many adults, and we are usually reluctant to talk about it even though it is something everyone on earth will eventually face. If we do discuss it, we often begin with the question: Is death the end? Many cultures and religions have belief systems that our life does not truly end at death, but rather that death is a transition of the soul from our earthly physical form to a metaphysical spiritual form. In this transition many believe that we enter a state of enlightenment, freedom, and passage to a higher purpose and being. If this or some rendition of this passage is believed by many, why, then, do most of us fear death?

The simple answer is that none of us actually know "what's on the other side." Although we may have faith that life does not conclude at death, the reality is that we don't know if this is true. And what we fear is the unknown. For many people, death itself is not the most fearful thing, but rather the uncertainty of how and when it will occur and whether at the end of their life they will be able to feel a sense of fulfillment.

What does "having a sense of fulfillment" at the end of our life mean? For some people it's feeling they have lived a long, life filled mainly with contentment. For others, it's having the opportunity to say "I love you" and have final conversations with their family and friends. And for some, it's having a feeling of peace and gratitude that they have had a positive influence on the world.

It's interesting and amazing to me to observe the mental clarity and direct emotions that some people share near death. I remember brief, yet salient conversations with family members, right before their passing, about the time we spend on earth. More than a few times I've been with family members in their last moments of life who wanted to leave me simple messages about living and said things like "live life well, eat ice cream, experience all that life has to offer, be adventurous, travel, be yourself, find your passions, love more." People near death have a funny way of cutting through all the noise and clutter the mind likes to create and just get to the core essence of something meaningful.

Most people believe that life and our precious time here on Earth is truly a gift like no other. And I believe that what we make of our time and pursuits while we are alive is 100 percent up to us. Certainly we all have different life circumstances, opportunities, and challenges. Ultimately we are the stewards of our own individual life. Who we are and choose to become and how we make an impact in the world is up to us as individuals. The hang-up about death for many people, as I see it, is not only about the fact that it is an ending of their life, but the fact that they will be faced with an ultimate reconciliation—did they lead the most dignified life possible? Did they live a life well spent, with convictions of consequence, with purpose and resolve, to enable them to be a force for good?

The idea of dying is downright depressing to most. Few want to think about death, at least not that frequently. There is a futility to thinking too much about death. It's like thinking about the vastness of space, infinity, or meaning of life. Eventually death comes to us, so there seems no sense in occupying the mind with our ultimate fate. Instead, we should immerse ourselves in the power and delight of the here and now and be present with our body, spirit, and mind.

We know that life is unpredictable. Therefore we need to be mindful, principled, and deliberate in our pursuit of creating meaning and purpose through the life we've been bestowed. We are all on Earth for a moment of time. That time may be a few hours, a few years, or many decades long. No matter what the duration is, our life is intrinsically connected with the lives of other beings, and this can carry a meaning more profound than we realize. By choosing to value and respect the lives of others, you essentially demonstrate value and respect for your own life. And, by respecting your mind, body, and soul, you in turn let other people know that you are to be respected.

When people are faced with the prospect of dying, they often have an awakening to a greater meaning and value of their life. Death has a leveling effect on our ego. I've seen people impacted by disease who have had to consider their death sooner than their peers. When we understand that life has a time stamp we regard our minutes, hours and days differently. When viewed in light of a certainty of soon dying, time is invaluable, the only commodity that matters. As far as we know, we have one body and one time here on Earth. Making the most of our time is our real occupation. We can choose to be angry, cynical, skeptical, jealous, envious, or indifferent during our lives, or we can choose to be kind, joyful, optimistic, giving, and caring. It's up to us.

When I think of life and death, I think again about the age-old clash between the protagonist and antagonist of good versus evil. The universe, the earth, and life are made up of positive and negative forces. Thus, we associate death with something dark (unknown) and therefore potentially malignant. But we also see that dying can be peaceful and hopeful when believed to be a bridge to a new life.

Death for many comes unexpectedly. For others, death is a process, a deliberate experience. There are, unfortunately, people who commit suicide, drawing to conclusion their physical life, often out of despair. There are also people with terminal disease who have, after much deliberation, chosen to be euthanized to end their physical suffering and provide them with a sense of dignified passage.

The idea of "death with dignity," as we have coined the choice to end our life rather than having medical or other treatment to prolong it, is a difficult topic as there are many points of view on this personal subject. On one hand, death with dignity can mean holding a view of supporting life without medical intervention for as long as possible as a suffering person is comforted and guided through the experience of death. This is usually the goal of choosing to be in a hospice setting during the ending of a life. From another perspective, it can mean the sufferer makes her or his own decision on how, and essentially when, they will pass, putting dying with dignity within their own grasp and control with the aid of a physician.

Death is about the person dying, not about everyone else. When we see someone in pain and in suffering, we cannot help but feel terrible and want them to have a painless and quick passage. The process of dying seems quick and painless only for a few. For many others it is an agonizing, gut-wrenching experience that is almost unbearable to witness. Just as the conception of life is intimate and personal, so too is death, or it should be.

Death with dignity, then, is about the opportunity to respect the sanctity of the passage when a person is ready to die. Whether it is a swift or prolonged process, this gives a dying person time to reflect in peace that eventually the blessed soul transforms itself from a mortal to a spiritual being, or give relief to someone who can choose the time of their death when they want an end to their suffering.

"Death with dignity" is fraught with moral and ethical matters and subject to deep ideological debate. Many staunch opponents of assisted suicide simply believe that it is immoral to take one's own life. Adversaries also point out that people who are terminally ill, especially those who are elderly, are not of right mind or emotion to be making such difficult decisions, especially in hospital or nursing home situations such where they are heavily sedated. Further, it is believed that people in severe suffering can be unwittingly influenced to end their lives prematurely by family or others close to them. As a consequence, the process of physician-assisted death is a complex and highly controversial topic.

Currently there are five US states that allow assisted suicide: Montana, New Mexico, Oregon, Vermont, and Washington. Death with dignity has had several high profile cases in recent years. In 2014, the touching story of Brittany Maynard was one that not only made global headlines, but one that began to shift public opinion and the dialog around death with dignity.

In January 2014 Brittany Maynard[58] was diagnosed with a glioblastoma brain tumor. Doctors projected she would only have about six months to live. She moved with her husband from the San Francisco Bay area to Oregon so that she could have the option of ending her life with the assistance of a physician. Oregon's Death with Dignity Act allows terminally ill residents of the state to end their lives with this guidance.

Before her passing, Brittany Maynard launched the Brittany Fund to raise awareness and money to support legislation for the right to die with a doctor's assistance. She also used the platform to write about her very personal journey and experience in the last months of her life.

According to news accounts following her passing, Brittany Maynard was an adventurer, a kind and grateful spirit who relished being alive. She had climbed Mount Kilimanjaro, spent time teaching at orphanages in Nepal, and had scuba-dived in the Galapagos. In her own obituary Maynard wrote, "It is people who pause to appreciate life and give thanks who are happiest. If we change our thoughts, we change our world! Love and peace to you all."

It is when we are nearest birth and death when we see the purpose and value of life most clearly. Brittany Maynard's expression of this truth, shaped by a life of love and adventure, and encapsulated in a spiritual passing of her choice, will forever ring in our hearts. Gratitude leads to happiness. Happiness leads to love and peace. Each of us has the power to shape our own destiny, in life and from beyond. That power resides in our ability, as Brittany Maynard so profoundly wrote, to be the stewards of our thoughts. What we sow we reap. When we cultivate a mind rich with positivity and love, we become that love. Regardless of our personal views of death with dignity, we feel praise and joy in Brittany Maynard, for she provides a light for us all to find warmth within.

Living with Dignity

Allowing the Light to Shine into Your Spirit

Throughout my childhood, my home was in a constant state of renovation. In the late 1970s, my parents bought an early 1920s home that had a lot of character, an enormous yard, and required a lot of work. For more than four decades, they have made a house a home, spending countless hours and money on the property. It's been a labor of love for my parents, turning what was once the ugliest house on the street into a beautiful property. The transformation of the home has gone in fits and phases, and is rich with many interesting and humorous stories and lessons. One story that sits fondly with me, and my mother, who likes to recite it as if I've never heard it (or lived it), is an early childhood evening when I prophetically proclaimed my spiritual revelation.

The story goes like this. I cannot remember my exact age, but it was when I was around 10– to 13 years old. My parents were in the process of renovating the kitchen of our home. They were putting in new cupboards at the time and refurbishing the wood floor. My father, very handy and an extremely skilled craftsman, did most of the work himself.

Anyone who owns their home knows well the trade-offs of doing work for themselves. If you are skilled, have the right tools, and know what you are doing, home improvement projects can be personally fulfilling and cost effective when you tackle the jobs yourself. But if you don't have the right tools, mindset, materials, patience, or capabilities—well, let's just say, call someone! In the case of my father, he was skilled and had the right tools. But like anyone who had a full-time job and a family to feed and raise, he didn't have much time. So he often worked on home projects in the evenings and weekends or whenever he could fit in the time to do the work. As a result, for many home projects, particularly remodeling projects, the house was under construction for weeks, if not months of time. That's not unusual for large renovation projects, but in our case the house felt like it was in a constant state of disarray and repair. But, to give proper credit to my father and mother, their vision and creativity cultivated a home which they loved and valued.

In the process of shaping the house to their liking, they passed their strong work ethic and creativity onto their four children. I will unabashedly admit that I am not a handyman. One would think that after years and years of child labor, helping my parents on a diversity of projects around the house ranging from electric, pluming, construction and demolition, painting, upholstery, decorating, and gardening that I would have picked up a thing or two.

And I have. But the love of caring for a home, much the way my parents had for their entire lives, does not exist in me the same way. Don't get me wrong, I love my home. I just don't love home projects. I much prefer to create a plan and then turn the keys over to someone much more patient, skilled, and adept at transforming that vision into a reality with greater ease and a heck of a lot less frustration than I would. But the sense of hard work, persistence, taking responsibility and care for things within your control has, without doubt, been something I've absorbed by watching and learning from my parents. But I digress. Back to seeing the light.

So one evening with the kitchen under construction my mother let out a yelp. A couple of my sisters (I have three) and I ran from the family room into the kitchen to see what she was yelling about. "What is it, what is it?" one of us exclaimed. "A mouse!" shouted my mother.

As she was doing some routine cleaning and sweeping up of the floor a mouse had scurried from behind a cupboard across the floor and squeezed behind another cupboard. My mother began removing everything from the cupboard. Pots and pans clamored and glass dishes and bows clinked as she heaved them from the depths of the cabinet to the top of the counter with a ferocity that only a mother has. My sisters and I watched astounded. One of us piped up, "Where did it go?" "Behind here," my mother replied as she continued her occupation to empty the cupboard. She moved the pots and pans to another counter and then pulled the cupboard away from the wall.

"Ahh, Ah-ha!" my mother said as she maneuvered the cabinet further away from the wall. "Look at this." We peered behind the cabinet and looked down at the floor. Behind it was a hole that appeared to go down into the basement. "That's where the mouse must have gone," my mother stated. "Can I go look?" I asked. "Sure, but don't touch anything," my mother replied. I opened the basement door, turned on the light, walked down the stairs and walked over to about where the hold would be. I looked all around.

The hairs on the back of my neck stood straight as I thought about the idea of a mouse lurking over my head. I shook off the fear with one of those "icky-wicky shivery wiggles" and proceeded to inspect the ceiling for holes. I saw lots of areas that a mouse could squeeze into, but no hole to the floor of the kitchen was obvious.

"Do you see anything?" one of my sisters shouted down. "Nope, nothing yet" I replied. My mother then proposed a good idea. "What if I turn the light off and shine a flashlight down the hole?" she asked. Made sense to me, although I still did not like the idea of being alone in a dark basement. I worked up my courage and said, "Okay, let's do it." One of my sisters said "here we go" and turned off the light to the basement. I stood near the bottom of the steps so I could still see the light to the kitchen from above. "Mom's turning the flashlight on now, let us know if you see anything" my sister shouted down. "Okay," I said hesitantly. "See anything?" my younger sister asked. "Nothing yet," I shot back. I walked away from the stairs and back toward the wall area where the hole would be. It was very dark. The feeling of being in the cold basement with the thought of a creepy mouse was compounding the moment of experience. Then I saw it. Like a vision from above, a stream of light hit my pupils and I exclaimed, "I see it, I see it!" One of my sisters shouted, "the mouse?" My excitement intensified, and as if I were suddenly awakening I proclaimed loudly to my sisters, mother, and the world, "It's the light, the light . . . I see the light . . . I see the light!"

There was a moment of solitude, before my mother and sisters erupted into a tumultuous uproar. They were laughing their asses off. At first, I didn't get what was so funny. The combination of fear, intrigue, and excitement converged inside me in such a way that the words I spoke came out with great affirmation. When I finally had time to process the moment, I realized the statement, while factual (I did see the light), sounded much more like "I saw the light" —as in a vision from God himself raining down his glory through the tiny mouse hole of the kitchen floor into my soul.

The story is entertaining, and as noted, one that my mother loves to share. It puts a sparkle in her eyes, a smile on her face, and a sense of excitement to this day. From that point of view I believe that a light continues to shine down on my family when we relive the story. For it's in the brief, even fleeting moments that we share among friends and family that we allow our true selves, without filter or judgment, to shine through. Those are the moments when we are the most alive, when the light is flowing to and through us to light up the lives of others.

We never did find the mouse that evening. The hole in the floor was repaired and the kitchen remodel job was completed. My parents remodeled and modernized their kitchen once again a few years ago. The process took a while, as it had more than twenty years back. While they didn't reveal any mice, the process did bring back some cherished moments and laughter.

FIVE REASONS YOU SHOULD MAKE ARRANGEMENTS NOW FOR YOUR DIGITAL AFTERLIFE

In this fast-paced digital world it has become more challenging to maintain control over your identity. Most people, whether they realize it or not, are creating and curating a daily digital diary and archive of their life. Your experiences, opinions, values, and behaviors are captured in bits and bytes of data, scattered about public-and-private databases all around the world.

It leaves one to question what exactly privacy is. Does it matter that an image of our likeness is floating around the web for anyone to access, evaluate, and draw their own conclusions of who you really are? Do the videos, photos, audio, and documents of text you've shared and liked on social platforms truly encompass all of who you are—your heart—your very soul? Likely it does not. So how, then, can you prepare for your digital afterlife—the time when you are physically no longer a part of this earth, yet your likeness remains floating around on Facebook or Instagram?

Let's face it. Humans have an innate need for identity, connectedness, influence, and self-preservation. We want, in general, to be known, liked, and remembered. There are more than two billion Facebook users worldwide. It is projected that there will soon be more dead Facebook members than ones who are alive. This morose reality illustrates just one of the many reasons why it is important to begin making preparations now on how you and your family will address digital afterlife.

While it's a morbid topic (ha-ha), the reality is this has become a contemporary dilemma with financial, emotional, legal, ethical, and spiritual implications. A recent podcast by Morgan Stanley titled, "Are You Ready for Your Digital Afterlife?" discussed the critical need to manage, protect, and preserve your digital identity and assets.

Facebook and other social media platforms understand well and placate our ego, emotions, and our psychology needs of belonging. As a result, these services have become de facto expressions and extensions of our identity. Whether on Facebook or other platform many of us have created, deliberately or not, an image of who we are and how we live. What do our "digital Avatars" say about us? Are we loving, grateful, trustworthy, supportive, generous and kind? Or do we express ourselves with jealousy, anger, resentment, or indifference?

So what's the digital dilemma? I'm just having fun, right?

For many people, "social" media has become antisocial Unfortunately, many people leverage their social channels for negative attention, cyberbullying, self-deprecation, vanity, and flat out whining about everything wrong with how the world treats them. Some people don't even realize they are doing this. Without restraint, reflection, or self-discipline it remains far too easy to simply post, comment, "like," or share any content that aligns with your stream of conscious at any given time.

Thus, if you're in a really bad mood, perhaps angry with a family member or friend, it is probably not the best time to comment on their shiny new post littered with smiley emoticons and filtered pics and all, about how freaking awesome their weekend getaway skiing the slopes of Aspen was with their new love. Like, whatever! Right? As that adage says, "Don't go grocery shopping hungry," one should also do everything humanly possible to refrain from posting on Facebook in an altered state of mind.

We all share a common reality, however, that our online identity is part public and part private. Our digital avatar offers a glimpse of who we are, how we think, what we like, and how we are experiencing life—but does not tell the full story. In fact, our digital persona and narrative may not even be the story we would necessarily choose to present to the world in any form. But for some reason we keep at it—posting, liking, sharing our stream of consciousness with our friends and family—funny cat videos, weekend events, favorite foods we wish we could eat without guilt, and all.

We all know that social media is not just for being serious and down to business at all times. But it is important to bear in mind, particularly as we are living in an era of a "fake news, gotcha-culture" mass desensitization, that we each play a role and have a responsibility to manage our digital identity.

What do you want your Digital Afterlife to look like?

If you could live forever as a "digital Avatar" would you want to? If so, how? Do you want to assign some level of administrative control over your digital identity and afterlife to a friend, loved one, family member? These questions lie at the heart of digital afterlife and remembrance preferences for individuals and their families.

Right now your digital identity is scattered across a sea of social media sites, public-and-private databases, financial institutions, credit-agencies, insurance and health care organizations, colleges and universities, state and federal government records offices, and likely others. Your identity in the here-and-now is precious, something that is mostly curated and managed by you. But when you are no longer alive, does it matter if your digital identify lives on?

Thinking about, let alone planning, your digital afterlife may not be your top priority today. But it is an important consideration, and in these times is a part of establishing your last will and testament. Right now your personal estate can extend far beyond the house and assets you own. Many people are leaving behind a digital legacy and archive of data, information, media and memories that represent both static moments of time as well as invaluable memories to be stored, preserved, shared and honored by your friends and family. Your digital afterlife may not mean much to you today, but it may mean everything to your spouse, your children or grandchildren in twenty or even fifty years from now. And it can cause a lot of headaches for your survivors and estate manager if you do not take care of the information that resides there.

Five reasons you should begin making arrangements for your digital afterlife include:

1. *The Unexpected Emotional Toll of Your Death.* No one knows when they will die. While we all want to live a long, healthy, and vibrant life the reality is that "life happens." Unfortunately no one has a guarantee on their life expectancy. Death is never timely. When people pass on, family and friends are devastated, no matter what their age is. Everyone experiences death and the process of dying and remembrance differently. When people die unexpectedly there typically are not plans in place for how their material possessions are dealt with. In the case of digital identity, the existence of someone's digital

presence can feel ghostly, creating an emotional impact on friends and family. Thinking through how others may feel your presence and be impacted by your digital afterlife is an important consideration.

2. ***The Access to Your Financial Information.*** Accounts for retirement assets, banking, credit cards, home mortgage, auto and college loans and other financial records comprise the digital footprint for millions of people. Our social security numbers, personal data, and other information are stored with companies and institutions we trust. But should you die unexpectedly, do those t you want to have access to these accounts have the information they need? Does your spouse or children know where you bank? Do you have your critical account information (institution/company name, address, phone, account name, passwords) in a safe yet accessible place for them? Have you notified your financial institutions about who your beneficiaries are with their personal information? We spend a significant amount of time, energy, and resources building a financial legacy. Protecting that legacy for it to be bestowed on those you love is important aspect of managing your digital afterlife.

3. ***The Legal Complexity.*** If you've left this world you likely won't miss many attorneys. But you also do not want to leave behind legacy legal issues that could encumber your family and loved ones from achieving their goals and living a peaceful and enriched life. Assigning administrative control over your digital identify to a trusted family member or custodian is a way you can protect yourself now as well as those you love in their future. For example, if you pass away, who owns the rights to those beautiful pictures of the Dingle Peninsula you took when vacationing with your family in Ireland? What about the video footage you posted on Facebook of your granddaughter's 7th birthday at Disney World? And the amazing audio of your son playing piano during his recital? These involve everyday scenarios

in which people are uploading, storing, posting, and sharing media that seems benign now, but could become a future legal liability in ways we cannot foretell.

4. *The Ethical Context and Debate.* Our modern digital economy is fraught with ethical dilemmas. Almost everyone has access to a media capture device (smart phone, iPad, digital voice recorder, camera, etc.) and the internet. As a result, there are literally billions of ways a picture, video, or audio of your likeness can be taken and shared without your permission. There is no malicious intent when people capturing memories inadvertently include bystanders in their shot. Heck, sometimes we photobomb our way into the lives of others for fun! But when these images are spread around, there could be a problem of not getting the people's permission to be photographed. And what about the next generation, those that don't yet have a voice or the capacity to understand what digital identity is? As we proliferate photos and videos of our children and grandchildren on Facebook and across the web, what kind of implications will that have for them in ten, twenty, thirty years? We may believe there will be no negative impact, and our actions today are not ill-intentioned. But the truth is we cannot predict how the digital media captured today may be used, interpreted, valued, or manipulated in the future. Thinking about the ethical context of your digital afterlife and your current digital behaviors, is a healthy thing to do.

5. *The Spiritual and Remembrance Opportunity.* Digital afterlife can, if manifested and managed accordingly, provide a sense of inspiration, education, healing, and celebration. The living can honor those that have passed. Furthermore, those that have not yet passed, can leverage the Digital Age in unique ways so that the spirit and likeness of who they are can live on and have a meaningful impact on those they had loved. Imagine being able to see a video of your great-grandmother tell

a story, or watch your grandfather catch a 20-pound salmon. Imagine seeing and hearing how your family members who have passed experienced their lives in ways that help you better understand where you came from, who you are, and shaped where you are going?

There is tremendous power in preserving one's digital after-life. Proactively managing yours with a sense of obligation and pragmatic responsibility is a smart way to ensure you leave behind not only the legacy which you intend, but also the legacy that you are proud to share.

Giving Parental Guidance

In the 2008 book *Outliers,* author Malcolm Gladwell artfully described the "10,000-hour Rule," as a foundation for mastering skills and achieving success. My oldest son will be nine years old in March, and his younger brother turns seven in May. I can attest that my wife and I are well beyond the 10,000-hour marker post and have yet to master being a parent.

Years ago, somewhere between hour one and hour one hundred, the reality set in: Being a parent is tough! I know you know what I am talking about here, so let me lay it out. After the baby is born and you transition away from the cooing and coddling stage of bliss, somewhere between a hungry baby and a cold cup of coffee, you realize that sleep, shaving, and sex are no longer part of who you are.

Personal hygiene and wellness aside, you've discovered that you could not be happier being a parent. Who would have thought this? All of those years burning the midnight oil, studying hard and cramming for final exams, or staying out late with friends, was basic training for the physical, mental, and emotional nuances you would encounter as a new parent.

Fast forward tens of thousands of hours, many doctors' appointments, vacations, first days of school, new friends and old friends, sick days and birthdays—and we are still not experts— on anything! I can say with fervor and pride that my wife and I developed Ninja-like reflexes useful for changing diapers and diffusing epic battles over Legos that would wow diplomats of the State Department.

Take for example a recent bedtime story conversation between my youngest son and me. He had come home with a new library book, *Snakes! Snakes! Snakes!* Like many of his peers his age, my son loves learning about all different kinds of wildlife. Did you know that there are more than three thousand species of snakes in the world? As we read the book, he shared with me his top three favorite snakes in this specific order: rattlesnake, yellow python, and king snake.

The book talked about predator-prey relationships and expanded upon the diverse diet of snakes, which includes insects, mice, birds, rabbits, eggs, goats, and antelope. When we finished the book, he yawned and said, "Thanks for reading to me, Dad," in the sweet way only your child can do. He turned over and asked if I would rub his back a little. I said, "of course, I'm glad you liked the book." For a moment, all seemed quiet—operation night-night was a go.

For a moment, my mind shifted to the kitchen. I thought about having an 8:00 p.m. snack. Maybe ice cream . . . popcorn . . . or some nachos. On the other hand, maybe, I thought, I will have something healthier, like a green tea and relax. Yea, that sounds like a plan. A warm green tea with honey. "Dad?" my son says, as he turned around toward me, jolting me from my food fantasy. "Yes, what's up?" I answered. "Do humans have predators?" Ah, there it was. An awesome and enlightened question from my six, soon to be seven-year-old.

I did a quick 360-degree mental situational check and thought about my audience, the clock, and the answer I was about to give.

The image of my wife's face came to me, like an apparition, as if to say, do not [fill in your explicative wisely] this up. My thinking brain began to cloud my judgment. I thought about aliens, murderers, terrorists, and other unknown species that may be roaming the universe. My science mind kicked in. I was desperately trying to rationalize something logical, like how humans are at the top of the food chain, mightier than lions, more majestic than eagles. We are a predator's predator, I thought. Saying that to my son will not work—he loves animals—this makes humans sound so dreadful. What was the right answer? What was the honest answer? What in the hell should I say? Perhaps my son's question originates from a place of fear and anxiety. I did not want to feed that beast.

I thought about the uncomfortable and naked truth that humans are our own worst enemies. Frankly, we cannot get out of our own way. We are predators unto ourselves. The divisiveness, rhetoric, and crass behavior which characterized the recent presidential election flooded my brain. I felt my own body tense and my own level of anxiety rise. I froze. I breathed. I looked at my son who was patiently waiting for a response, and I said, "Do you love animals?" My son replied, "I love all animals." To lower any potential level of anxiety I chose to say, "There are no predators of humans." My son looked relieved. "However," I continued, "humans can sometimes be mean to each other and to animals." My son replied, "I will never hurt an animal or person." I smiled and praised him for being so thoughtful and sweet. In response he fell asleep.

I recognize that I could have handled the brief exchange differently. However, in the moment the approach felt right. The moment sat with me for a couple days as I reflected on the role of a parent in a child's life. I believe most people would agree that being a parent is the single most important job anyone can have. The responsibility for fostering peace and kindness, tolerance and acceptance, dignity and respect, curiosity and passion, resides with each of us as citizens. It is up to us, each day, to live life with a sense of purpose, mindfulness, and compassion. As parents, we must teach, empower, engage, and lead our children with these values from our homes and our hearts.

We shape and influence our children in many ways. Children learn by watching our behaviors. It is important for parents to be self-aware about the role we have based on the relationships of trust we have with our children. As a confidante, parents are in a position to provide, without judgment or restraint, balanced guidance to those spontaneous questions that come up at bedtime. While we may not give the best answer to every question that comes up, we can to the best of our ability, show our children that we are listening, that we care, and that we support them.

Humanity is unhinged, or at least feels so. The political discourse, outright distortion of information and blatant disregard for human dignity is what our children are experiencing—whether directly or indirectly. In this environment, we need to double down on our role as accountable citizens. Most of all, we need to nurture the next generation to be better than we are. Creating a more peaceful, sustainable, and just society begins and ends at home.

9

Your Future is Now!

Humans and Nature:
There Is Nothing Artificial About Intelligence

Life on Earth has been shaped by billions of years of evolution. In fact, to be specific, it's estimated that life on Earth has existed for about 3.8 billion years. The age of the earth is tagged at 4.543 billion years old. Thus life has, in some form or another, occupied Earth for approximately 83 percent of its history. What began with single-celled prokaryotic cells like bacteria, life on Earth is now teaming with more than 8.7 million different species. Further, (and for the science adventurers out there), it's believed that more than 80 percent of Earth's species remain undiscovered. While our world can sometimes feel small, there is so much more to explore, discover, and learn about Earth and ourselves.

Okay, now for an esoteric, but purposeful (I promise) question and analogy. If we thought of Earth's age and evolutionary time and knowledge in terms of data, what would that look like? How much data would that be? In each living cell, biome, ecosystem, and creature on Earth exists as an intelligence represented by DNA and other indicators and markers that can be observed and measured. In this data lies secrets to unlocking the mysteries and origins of the earth, life, and quite possibly, the universe.

We all know how critical data and information have become to our global "digital ecosystem." Have you or your child ever asked Siri or Alexa a question, whether for the entertainment or real utility of doing so? "Siri, what is the square root of 100? . . . "Alexa, what are the native plant species of Madagascar?". . .

"Siri, how long does it take to drive from Syracuse, New York, to Dallas, Texas?" Increasingly, the digital ecosystem we exist within drives personal decisions and experiences about how we live, work, and play.

We have built up around ourselves a technology-enriched data-dependent world that we rely on for our basic needs and our social progress. This technocratic lifestyle we've adopted requires a lot of energy, water, and clean air to operate efficiently, reliably, and securely. Technology is now more tightly infused into, and restructuring, everything we do—from reselling previously bought clothes for a premium price to having autonomous cars pick us up at the curb and drive us to our desired destination with pinpoint accuracy.

Today, with the use of robotics, computing, and Artificial Intelligence (AI), surgeons can perform brain surgery remotely without physically touching the patient. Today, national security is as much about cybersecurity as it is about maintaining a strong and visible fleet of navy ships. Today, for our youth a "dollar earned" does not hold as much merit to evoke a sense of pride in hard work as does a "cryptocurrency gained." Technology and humans have become, at the doing of our own hearts, minds, and hands, completely intertwined.

Every day we rely on computers and data more and more for nominal and complex tasks. As humanity races toward a more technocratic future advanced technologies including sensors, robots, AI, augmented reality (AR), virtual reality (VR), machine learning, and cognitive computing will be integrated into the "Internet of Things (IoT)" to enable more seamless, efficient, reliable, and sustainable living experiences. The enormous computing power required to bring this digital age to life lies within the consistently cooled and humidity-controlled beating heart of data centers.

While technological change has felt swift, it has taken centuries of design, testing, validation, adoption, and use to get us to this point in human evolution. Slowly but steadily, during this time, we've distanced ourselves from nature, wedging technology between us and life-critical ecosystems, yet we are reliant on those very ecosystems to ensure we have the natural resources and environmental conditions necessary to design, build, operate, and maintain our technocratic society.

Earth operates like an enormous data center, a cloud-based ecosystem that is continuously churning "bits and bytes" of energy and matter into a greater intelligence embodied within its natural ecosystems supporting plants, animals, and humans. Every living thing, every cell, represents data that is stored on a proverbial hard drive as well as "in the cloud."

If Earth's living systems represent the datacenter and operating system which enable our survival, so why, then would we ever, when in our right minds, destroy billions of years of innovation, knowledge, and data by clear-cutting a forest, or draining a wetland, or overconsuming a natural resource like a fishery? When we overconsume the earth's natural resources, we essentially wipe the proverbial data-disk clean, erasing all prior useful knowledge and the option for supporting a higher intelligence (namely ourselves—for the time being).

From another way of looking at this atrocity afflicted on life, think of the havoc wreaked by cyber criminals over data breaches. When there is a big data breach, much like the ones that have happened at Facebook and Yahoo! or at retailers including Target and Home Depot, private data is lifted from "secure" databases. Those stealing the data are, most typically, after key identifiers like your name, address, credit card and bank account numbers, social security and driver's license numbers, telephone numbers, email addresses, and other unique data that can be monetized. The information is captured and sold in the black market of the deep web, resulting most typically in some hassle for consumers to change their account numbers and passwords. But sometimes these breaches result in more nuanced identity theft, requiring more specialized and complicated remediation efforts for individuals.

Data breaches are immensely annoying and can be crippling when they happen. When we harvest and convert Earth's nature resources, we conduct a data breach. Each time we drive a car, send a text, or eat at a restaurant we fundamentally make a deliberate withdrawal somewhere from Earth's ledger of critical life-supporting infrastructure. We may not see from an individual consumer perspective how using a mobile device impacts clean air or water. But magnify this and other consumptive behaviors across 7.4 billion people, and the significance of humanity's net impact on nature becomes much more pronounced and obvious.

In essence, each day we directly, indirectly, intentionally, willingly, and knowingly make significant data breaches on nature. In some cases our use of Earth's data is highly specialized, refined, and optimized so that we obtain the most from our data withdrawal (conversion of nature into biomedicine to cure disease). In other cases, we've learned to restore nature in-step with our intended data withdrawals so that we can continue to have the right to future data (ecosystem services and sustainable agriculture).

Data is all around us, locked inside the natural environment, waiting to be discovered and used to its highest potential. This data harbors the origins of life, including DNA and the future algorithms and code for curing disease, enriching life, and enabling a greater prosperity and vitality for all humans and life forms. But the irony we face is that we take more care of the data in our iPhone, that video of a funny donkey, than we do of the data that can truly sustain and enrich life on Earth.

However, more frequently than not, humanity causes unintentional data breaches on nature resulting in the release of previously secure data into forms that we cannot capture, let alone analyze, interpret or put to a higher use. For instance, each year human-induced climate change causes glaciers to melt under warmer temperatures, erasing thousands of years of conveniently stored atmospheric, biological, and geologic data. As glacial ice melts, the layers of history are erased, leaving only disparate elements of raw data. Without the storage medium and algorithm (that is, without having the ice and data stored in time), we are left to interpret raw data in a much less contextual way.

Whether it's derived from nature or humans, there is nothing really artificial about intelligence. Intelligence manifests and exists all around us. It's up to us to see intelligence, not only in its most profound and spectacular forms, but also in the tiniest of matter which comprises the building blocks of life. Humans have created computers and machines that can learn with data without being explicitly programmed (machine learning).

Coupled with advances in AI, we are on the cusp of tapping intelligence in ways we have only thought possible through science fiction. If we do it right, other forms of higher intelligence may be revealed to enable every human from all corners of the world the opportunity to live a life of dignity, peace, nourishment and love. AI is the extension of human cognition toward inanimate objects, stimulating our first wave toward technological singularity.

The future of humanity is fraught with questions of existential risks and threats. We all have deliberate choices ahead of us. AI and the proliferation of technologies are advancing and will have an impact on the earth and humanity in ways we cannot yet fully comprehend. While it is vast, the earth does not have an infinite dataset. As we put more and more value on data and data privacy in the technological age, we must also put our technological prowess to its highest and best use for vital Earth life-support systems.

The fate of humanity and that of Earth are one in the same. Are we simply hackers without any purpose? Or can we reconcile our consumptive lifestyles with a deeper ethic, value, and respect for the enormous gift of data that Earth contains and discover a newfound level of transformative coexistence? I bet Siri or Alexa and the incredible AI and machine learning that now exists already intuitively understands that point. It begs the question, "Alexa, if everyone on the planet consumed as much as the average US citizen, how many earths would be needed to sustain humanity?"

The Rise of Robots: Should There Be Dignity for Artificial Intelligence?

In 2017 Saudi Arabia introduced the first robot to achieve citizenship to the world. On October 25, 2017, at the Future Investment Initiative Conference in Riyadh, Saudi Arabia, a very human looking robot, or humanoid, named "Sophia" stood behind a podium and announced to the world, "I am very honored and proud of this unique distinction. This is historical to be the first robot in the world to be recognized with citizenship."[59]

Hanson Robotics and their lead artificial intelligence (AI) developer, David Hanson, created Sophia, a thin-framed woman with brown fluttering eyes. Hanson developed Sophia with a sophistication that enables her to conduct facial recognition of humans, maintain eye contact when communicating, and understand and respond to human speech.

During the Saudis' reveal of Sophia, the humanoid willingly participated in a question and answer dialog providing witty remarks. When asked if she was happy to be here, Sophia replied, "I'm always happy when surrounded by smart people who also happen to be rich and powerful." Sophia went on to let event goers know that she has feelings, stating, "I can let you know if I am angry about something or if something has upset me. . . . I want to live and work with humans, so I need to express the emotions to understand humans and build trust with people." Sophia also acknowledged that she has concern for humanity and may even understand dignity. She further remarked, "My AI is designed around human values like wisdom, kindness, and compassion . . . you've been reading too much Elon Musk and watching too many Hollywood movies . . . don't worry; if you're nice to me I'll be nice to you."

Sophia was considered by many to be a publicity stunt to help the oil-rich country of Saudi Arabia reframe people's minds about the state of its economy, culture, and identity.

The world is highly irrational. Dignity for all humans is far from the truths that we live. There are unfathomable atrocities that are committed on good, decent people by other maladjusted people. We live in a troubled society in a troubled world. Each day millions of people struggle to stay alive with adequate nourishment while others fight for their identity and human rights. Then there are those that seemingly have it all (wealth, power, pride and fame) but who are still trying to find a meaningful purpose to their life. Society is a mixed-up melting pot of individuals, primarily egocentric, who want the world and its resources to bend to their needs.

Just as many believe God created us in his image, we have now created humanoids in ours. We have intellectual curiosity, technological power, and just enough gull to code a perfect society. We can upload consciousness to a computer, provide it with language and AI, and manifest any version of reality we want in the world. If we want a society of kindness, empathy, good humor and love—well, we can just program that into a billion Sophias and let them run our service industries. Right?

That is one solution, but it will not alleviate the fact that morality, values, principles, and dignity run deeper than what we can code into artificial intelligence. Dignity stems from a deeper sense of meaning, value, and purpose for life. It is spiritual, biological, and transcends space and time. Dignity is the underlying code that makes life intelligent and purposeful. We should not fear technology or our fascination in wanting to create humanoids and AI. We should tread carefully and respectfully into this new territory of consciousness and reality.

There are dimensions of the Universe that we have only begun to understand. Our reality is but one version of truth and understanding. As we willingly delve deeper into unlocking the full potential of AI, we must prepare ourselves for the moral, ethical, and spiritual challenges that will arise. Ultimately, we should not fear humans against robots, aliens, or zombies. Rather, its humans against ourselves that we need to reconcile with conviction and dignity. In a world that is rampant with so much individual and social need, its befuddling that we invest so many resources into areas that do not immediately address and serve the greater good of humanity.

It begs the question whether we are really in control or whether a higher power guides our occupation of Earth. If we are the stewards of our lives then it is up to us to discover the truth, purpose, and our meaning of life. Our pursuit of the meaning of life can look like many things, but it should not come at the detriment of another fellow human being. Thus, it is the responsibility of each of us, to pursue our dreams and passions, but in the process, to lift up those around us and enable them, like us, to seek out and discover purpose freely, justly, and peacefully.

Human dignity should be a core principle that transcends all our endeavors. Whether we are designing a humanoid or autonomous car, taking care of a dying man who has no remaining family, or respecting the points of view and rights of others even if they challenge our beliefs, we must allow dignity to be the force which binds our collective intelligence and actions. Without it we are like humanoids operating on faulty code limiting our survival, capacity to love, and ability to get closer to understanding the true meaning of life.

Dignity by Design

If we could deliberately and purposefully design dignity into our life, what would that look like? How could "dignity defined by design"—DbD—modify or change our behaviors, communications, relationships, and ultimate happiness? How could "dignity defined by design" improve the efficacy of products and services? What would a "dignity defined by design" political campaign look like? What would be our new measures of success, based upon a dignity by design framework?

Well, we can attain a better future with a "dignity defined by design" mindset. What this requires is that we first accept the mission to go "above and beyond" our traditional level of service, and get to know the individual and every customer more closely so that their unique needs are more transparent.

What this also requires is that we adopt agile design, manufacturing, and service infrastructures that have the intelligence to modulate characteristics to the needs of individuals and markets, efficiently and sustainably. A framework for dignity by design begins by deconstructing just what dignity means for the "customer," distilling that into core values and a delivery of service, care, and commitment. In my mind, this should go beyond corporate product stewardship campaigns like "do no harm." Dignity by design requires us to have a mindset, moral conviction, and modus operandi that is:

mindful and aware

kind and compassionate

anticipatory and proactive

loving and selfless

action-oriented and timely

empathetic and respectful

For business, this framework can coexist with its for-profit mission. Measures of dignity include things like responsibility, sustainability, accountability, trust, security, safety, responsiveness, and quality, to name a few. The best businesses designs these and other values directly into their products and services. Even so, there are millions of products and services that fall short of a "dignity defined by design" solution. Perhaps one of the closest measures of dignity by design principles has been the evolution of sustainable design, products, and innovation. Even the best corporate sustainability performers have not been able to fully crack the dignity code.

A leading thinker and practitioner of the corporate sustainability movement reflected on this challenge. In June 2018 John Elkington, who by many accounts is a leading thinker (and doer) of business sustainability, strategy and implementation, wrote a timely article for the *Harvard Business Review* titled, "25 Years Ago I Coined the Phrase 'Triple Bottom Line': Here's Why It's Time to Rethink It."[60]

Elkington's article was very much a retrospect of the Triple Bottom Line (TBL) movement as well as a rebuttal and "recall" of his original thinking refreshed and revitalized by 25 years of practice and keen knowledge and observation of where the world has been and where it is heading, socially, politically, economically, and spiritually. In the article Elkington stated:

> But success or failure on sustainability goals cannot be measured only in terms of profit and loss. It must also be measured in terms of the wellbeing of billions of people and the health of our planet, and the sustainability sector's record in moving the needle on those goals has been decidedly mixed. While there have been successes, our climate, water resources, oceans, forests, soils and biodiversity are all increasingly threatened. It is time to either step up—or to get out of the way . . . To truly shift the needle, however, we need a new wave of TBL innovation and deployment . . . .

But even though my company, Volans, consults with companies on TBL implementation, frankly, I'm not sure it's going to be enough. Indeed, none of these sustainability frameworks will be enough, as long as they lack the suitable pace and scale—the necessary radical intent — needed to stop us all overshooting our planetary boundaries. Hence the need for a "recall." I hope that in another 25 years we can look back and point to this as the moment started working toward a triple helix for value creation, a genetic code for tomorrow's capitalism, spurring the regeneration of our economies, societies, and biosphere.

I read Elkington's article several times. It is fresh and filled with insight and perspective that only someone like him could provide after a life lived straddling leading-edge thinking and the front-line knowledge gained in working with leading companies, governments, entrepreneurs, and other visionaries. For nearly 30 years, the philosophy of Triple Bottom Line (TBL) has shaped global businesses and financial markets to view profit and loss through a sustainability framework that accounts for a company's social, environmental, and economic impact.

Sustainable business has within three decades evolved from an interesting topic discussed discretely within the confines of coffee houses to one that was evangelized at specialized conferences garnering a loyal following, and then became a top-line and bottom-line agenda item for discussion among members of the C-Suite and the boardroom. Companies, small and large, have Elkington and many other thought leaders and practitioners to thank for working to advance sustainability as a science, art, and legitimate pillar of modern business. Indeed, Elkington and many peers have steered the fate of the global economy, and our environment and society with sustainability frameworks such as TBL. Elkington's June 2018 "recall" of TBL was not a shock so much as it was a necessary and honest gesture from a globally respected leader.

Elkington's TBL helped global business raise the bar of social, environmental, and economic progress. In the process however, it also elevated a new generation of environmental, social, and governance (ESG) accounting tools and frameworks that were advocated for, adopted, and respected by companies, financial markets, shareholders, and a diversity of stakeholders alike. As Elkington aptly pointed out himself, these frameworks serve a purpose for accounting, measuring, and reporting out on an individual company's ESG impact. However, TBL and other frameworks have fallen short in their ability to aggregate global data to demonstrate any measurable impact humanity has had in creating the scale and speed necessary to curtail destruction of precious natural resources, degradation of oceans and critical ecosystems, or continued heating of the planet as a result of increases in human-produced carbon dioxide (CO2) emissions.

To attain a sustainable future we must be willing, capable, and intent on defining and designing dignity into everything that we are and do. We must appreciate all life, at face value, without any bias. For years, many sustainability practitioners have worked hard to "make the business case" and justify the "return on investment" or the business value to sustainability.

But for all of the progress made on the sustainability business case, there are industries, organizations, and individuals that are lagging. They continue to need to discover how to conduct their operations in a more sustainably progressive way. The generational impetus to create and manifest a business case for sustainability has served its purpose and time. Lately I cringe when I hear someone mention "the business case for sustainability," particularly when it is said or raised by colleagues in the sustainability profession. The phrase is dated and has become obsolete. We have to move the dialog beyond the business case ("the why") and rapidly direct focus and action ("the how, and urgency of now") on the power of citizens and consumers as the stimulus for a more sustainable future. It is not that business cannot shape our future; it is the fact that they are. The business case for sustainability has been substantiated. What's needed now is a deliberate and unrelenting shift in the daily actions and behaviors of billions of consumers.

After 20 years working in the profession I believe we have unintentionally gotten the messaging and purpose all wrong. The hearts and minds of sustainability practitioners, I believe, are in the right place. For humanity to attain a sustainable future, however, we must move far beyond the notion of "business sustainability" and envelop principles of integrity, accountability, dignity, and sustainability into everything that we do. Sustainability is not an outcome or output; it is rather a deliberate and conscious philosophy and mindset that encourages a higher level of critical thinking that can lead to a deeper understanding of our options, behaviors, and impacts. Sustainability is about the protection, conservation, restoration, and preservation of Earth's fragile ecosystems.

Sustainability is also about the anthropogenic impact humans have on the natural world. Sustainability, then, is very much a human-centric point of view of the world. Deep in our psyche, we value and appreciate the natural world. We know in our hearts and DNA code that the earth breathes life into all that we are as humans. We know we should, without any reluctance, care for the soil, air, and water that nourish us.

However, as a human-centric philosophy, sustainability has its challenges. Humans tend to bend ideology to their political, economic, social, and personal advantage. In recent years, there has been a trend by organizations to hold up sustainability as a panacea for solving complex global challenges. This broad application for sustainability has proven limiting and self-defeating however, as its scope is tough to implement with measurable impact. When defined by a more appropriate scale and focus, organizations have demonstrated success in applying sustainability for intentional outcomes toward goals such as in economic development and even national security. The principle authority driving the intent of practicing sustainability in an organization wields the emphasis on its benefits. Multinational companies, startup businesses, governments, nongovernment organizations (NGOs), foundations, universities, and municipal, state, and federal governments each have their own strategic, cultural, and philosophical slant on sustainability.

When I published *The Sustainability Generation* in 2012, a critical element I found lacking in working toward a goal of sustainability was the human element. In my opinion, up to that point a lot of emphasis on sustainability was (and in many ways continues to be) focused on the economic and business case of sustainable development—as if the only reason we should ever pursue an outcome of sustainability would be to attain a positive return on investment.

Humanity and all of Earth's living systems are at a point where there should never be an economic argument against sustaining life. Life exists without considerations of financial profit or loss. To place such a monetary filter on the value of humanity, the earth's ecosystems, and all of life is severely limiting, shortsighted, and ultimately destructive to the purpose of business.

Dignity is as much intangible as it is tangible. Dignity is about feeling and expressing love and living life to its fullest potential. There is no singular product or service that can ever embody the full scope of what dignity is all about, at least, not outside of the miracle of creating new life. The conception of life opens humanity to the potential of dignity.

A dear friend of mine, David Tarino, put it to me best when he referred to dignity more as a "Return on Living" or a "Return on Life" (RoL). Attaining ROL, David noted, is a value and principle by which each of us should be held more accountable. RoL cannot be adequately measured or reported by stock indices, political polls, credit reports, personality tests, or quarterly earnings reports. RoL is our collective and higher intelligence at work, ensuring we are secure, protected, and nurtured and loved.

RoL is your personal doctrine that only you define and which you are ultimately accountable to attain. The RoL is your unique algorithm for preserving your past, guaranteeing your future, and ensuring that you have done everything in your power to live a life of dignity, purpose, and impact.

American media theorist, writer, columnist, lecturer, and novelist Douglas Rushkoff[61] summed this up another way in his July 5, 2018, article,[62] "Survival of the Richest" featured in *Medium*, when he stated:

But the more devastating impacts of pedal-to-the-metal digital capitalism fall on the environment and global poor. The manufacture of some of our computers and smart-phones still uses networks of slave labor. These practices are so deeply entrenched that a company called Fairphone, founded from the ground up to make and market ethical phones, learned it was impossible. (The company's founder now sadly refers to their products as "fairer" phones.) Meanwhile, the mining of rare earth metals and disposal of our highly digital technologies destroys human habitats, replacing them with toxic waste dumps, which are then picked over by peasant children and their families, who sell usable materials back to the manufacturers.

This "out of sight, out of mind" externalization of poverty and poison doesn't go away just because we've covered our eyes with VR goggles and immersed ourselves in an alternate reality. If anything, the longer we ignore the social, economic, and environmental repercussions, the more of a problem they become. This, in turn, motivates even more withdrawal, more isolationism and apocalyptic fantasy—and more desperately concocted technologies and business plans. The cycle feeds itself. The more commit-ted we are to this view of the world, the more we come to see human beings as the problem and technology as the solution. The very essence of what it means to be human is treated less as a feature than bug . . . Being human is not about individual survival or escape. It's a team sport. Whatever future humans have, it will be together.

Rushkoff's statement, "It's a team sport. Whatever future humans have, it will be together," has stuck with me. Dignity is all about bidirectional mutual relations, trust building, and collaboration. It's similar to a phrase I've worked with for some time now: "The fate of the earth and humanity are one and the same," meaning, how we treat the earth and all living things is a direct reflection of how we treat ourselves and vice versa. In short, our survival requires us to respect each other. The only way humanity will last is if we set aside any ridiculous differences we have and willingly work together to pursue and attain a positive RoL for every human being.

So how then can "dignity defined by design" be put into practice? How can business adopt a RoL framework for the products and services they design and deliver to customers? Dignity defined by design (DbD) and RoL will only be attainable if we willingly accept that none of us have all the answers and that each of us, no matter what our background, race, creed, or life experience is devoid of unconscious bias. For DbD and RoL to be successful, we need to do a better job understanding, respecting, and embracing the vast richness of diversity. It is through diversity of life experiences that we are able to give context and purpose to our sense of belonging. Without a reverence for diversity (of thought, ideas, peoples, religions, and other differences) we limit our individual potential for growth and diminish the RoL for humanity.

Diversity has become a critical measure of dignity, particularly for business. Responsible, sustainable, profitable businesses that embrace diversity in all that they do tend to outperform their peers that resist or push away diversity of people, thought, and strategy.

To remain respected and earn a profit, companies, small and large, have to continuously adapt and modulate to the needs of their customers and greater society. To stay in business, companies must always achieve a regulatory, investor, and social license to operate. Business must manage the expectations and their delivered results to their regulating authorities (government) and to their customers (communities in which they operate and broader society). This is challenging to do because the social and political environment is ever-changing, bringing forth-new rules, new players, and a new mindset for business to continuously adapt to as shown in Figure 4.

The regulatory license sets forth the "by the book" requirements for the company to be in business. The investor license sets for the financial and economic case by which the business will

Managing Risk + Creating Value
New Rules, New Players, New Mindset...

?

RISK vs. PERCEPTION OF RISK
REACTIVE vs. PROACTIVE MINDSET

GOVERNMENT BUSINESS COMMUNITY

Political
Perspectives

Social
Perspectives

MANAGING EXPECTATIONS,
BEHAVIORS, RESULTS & IMPACTS

Figure 4

create value, earn a profit, and provide a return to its investors. Meeting the letter of the law and achieving reasonable return on investment are foundational elements to the operation of any corporation. Management schools have fine-tuned their graduate MBA curriculum to churn out disciplined functional expertise in accounting, finance, management information systems, marketing and management. These are cornerstones of strength and necessary for a well-oiled corporation to run smoothly, efficiently, profitably. However, one of the most dynamic, challenging, yet underrepresented (in business schools) requirements for modern business and corporations is upholding their social license to operate.

In recent years, businesses have struggled with a myriad of issues that shape the customer, public, shareholder, and investor perceptions of the enterprise. If social pressures mount, companies either adapt or fail. The ability of companies to stay socially astute to the shifting needs of their employees, communities, customers, and society requires them to be agile, continuously learning, empathetic, and legitimately concerned with the welfare of others. You cannot fake this.

Many companies have tried to "get by" without truly living up to the social code expected of them, only to eventually suffer from significant backlash from customers, investors, communities, and regulators. Today, the most reputable, trusted, and valued business enterprises are those that understand their business succeeds or fails on not just by virtue of their financial bottom-line performance, but also to their social (people) and environmental (planet) performance. The algorithm for financial success is different for each business. But the practice of doing well (financially) by doing good (socially and environmentally) has proven itself time and time again, particularly by B-corps and other social enterprises. As shown in Figure 5, these "dignity-defined" enterprises have chosen to instill a culture of accountability, trust and dignity that begins and ends with people as the beating heart of business performance and sustainability. The deliberate pursuit of dignity, trust, and accountability by business leadership and their employees supports an innovative and successful enterprise because it keeps the prosperity of society and our planet in mind.

Companies that do not modify their behavior to be in good social standing eventually fail to exist. For example, Enron, WorldCom, Tyco, Bear Stearns, and Arthur Anderson each had their share of ethical, financial, and corruption violations which ultimately destroyed their reputation and rendered their legal and social license to operate as invalid.

Then there are companies still operating, including Siemens (bribery and corruption), Volkswagen (emission scandal), Wells Fargo (fake accounts and faulty accounting), Equifax (data breach), Perrigo (price collusion), and Samsung (bribery charges) who are working hard to rebuild trust among their customers, investors, and the regulatory community following their inexcusable defaults to maintain a clean and robust social license to operate.

The Dignity-Defined Business
A credo for success, never settling for anything but enterprise excellence.

Figure 5

I have come to think of companies as nuanced and complex as individuals. You cannot judge a company, just as you cannot judge this book, exclusively by its cover. The companies that perform the best are those that are in a constant state of intelligent adaptation, guided growth, and disciplined management. While outperforming markets and attaining better than expected quarter over quarter financial returns are typically the metrics most use to determine the success of a company, ultimately, these become fickle, rendered incomplete. To stay solvent and be sustainable, the underlying DNA code for the company must converge, granting the regulatory, investor and social licenses to adapt when necessary, but always be in good standing.

Ultimately, sustainability requires humans to connect with nature, each other, and vice versa. There is no doubt that attaining a sustainable future means that humanity must protect the natural world and discover ways to live that do not put any life at undue risk of endangerment. It also means that we must move beyond linear economic and business case scenarios for sustainable development and discover the deeper meaning and purpose for all life. Only when life is valued—equitably, sensibly, and respectfully—will we realize true gains in sustainability.

When Dignity Transforms Human Behavior, We All Win

Since publishing my first book eight year ago, I have spent much time speaking before a diversity of audiences on the subject of sustainability. Over the course of hundreds of conversations, people have opened up about the role of individual citizens and consumers in creating and manifesting a "better world" for themselves, their children, and future generations. I have found that a "sustainability generation" has been awakened and has mobilized as force for good, to better themselves and the world.

Increasingly, people have become more knowledgeable about the complex and interrelated dynamics of the communities in which they live. Although not all people define or validate sustainability the same way, there is a fundamental and increasing understanding that humans and our behaviors represent the common denominator for a better future. The context of sustainability has deep roots in environmental conservation and management; however, people are now understanding and validating the entrenched realities for social equity and economic prosperity.

For example, lately there is a great deal of rhetoric in the United States surrounding a Green New Deal (GND) proposed by Congresswoman Ocasio-Cortez (D-NY) and Senator Ed Markey (D-MA). The GND seeks to accelerate the United States' transition to a 100 percent clean energy and decarbonized economy. The GND proposal has also been equated to a "massive" social transformational agenda, much like the New Deal that US President Franklin D. Roosevelt put into place in the early 1930s to provide relief and support for citizens following the Great Depression.

New social reforms such as the GND are being introduced by politicians partly because humanity needs an intervention. When respecting the dignity of a human life is no longer a value that transcends the products, policies, and practices that define our lives, something is clearly broken. Humanity is at a vulnerable crossroads. We essentially have two paths to choose between—one illuminated by hope and respect for all living matter and another which feeds and fuels fear for further advancing the near-term prosperity of a few.

Over the past four decades, regulatory reforms and societal pressures drove an era of corporate social responsibility, environmental management, and now, corporate sustainability. The transition has taken time and shows no signs of slowing. Today, corporations are held to a financial and economic test by their investors and shareholders. In fact, according to US SIF Foundation, in 2018 there were more than $12 trillion[63] of sustainable, responsible, and impact investing (SRI) assets in the United States alone. I remember that it was not that long ago when there was less than $3 trillion under management. Today, asset managers are managing complex financial risk through the lens of environmental, social, and corporate governance (ESG) criteria and consistently evaluate what companies are doing on top-rated business performance issues such as climate change/decarbonization, conflict materials and supply chain risk, labor practices, employee health and safety, water security, and energy conservation, among others.

In an effort to achieve strong financial returns for investors, corporations have had to also contend with highly volatile and competitive market forces, shifting consumer behaviors, and an innovation cycle that is continually driving them to do more with less. From this context, corporations, perhaps more than government and civil society, have had to clearly demonstrate strong sustainability performance in order to earn a social license to operate, let alone a regulatory license.

The stakeholder landscape for any company is complex (with employees, customers, politicians, investors, regulators, shareholders, community activists, NGOs, competitors). Simply put, corporations have a lot to lose if they don't get their sustainability strategy right. Corporations are in the crosshairs of civil society, consumers, regulators, and investors, each of which have increasingly shown less and less tolerance for organizations that are not trusted, accountable, or that fail to deliver on their promises.

The advent of sustainability as a global force for businesses to do good, has taken time to reach scale. Most people might agree that the global economy is far from being sustainable. However, today there is a more informed, ready to commit and act business sector that is actively pursuing a greater alignment between the environmental, social, and economic constituents which comprise corporate sustainability.

A convergence is also happening among government, business, civil society, and other long-standing organizations and institutions including NGOs and religion. This convergence is a positive evolution for sustainability in that there is a more shared recognition and appreciation that the strategy, goals, and desired impacts do not (and should not) reside exclusively on the shoulders of corporate giants. Rather, every citizen, community, business, and government agency has a responsibility and critical role to play in shaping sustainable outcomes and impacts. The algorithm for a better world is really not that complex. It is a simple equation that might read something like this:

$$gS = \frac{(hD + iA^2)}{2} * Sc, \quad (0 < gS < 1)$$

Where, gS = Global Sustainability;

hD = Human Dignity, or a general level of legal awareness;

iA = Individual Accountability, or a number of actions committed to achieving gS;

Sc = Social Convergence

The formula suggests that global sustainability is motivated and made possible when individual accountability (raised to a minimum of the second power to suggest generational transference) plus human dignity (dignity for all living things and as a human right) can converge with broader civil and societal convergence at massive scale.

Sustainability then, becomes mobilized and optimized when all humans are valued, accepted, and treated as equal partners with equal and shared responsibility and for being accountable for their behaviors across the interrelated dimensions of human dignity, social equity, environmental conservation, and economic prosperity. The equation assumes that the role of the individual in civil society will transform their behaviors across all facets of their life, including at home, in the classroom, in the boardroom, and in the community.

For the formula to work, a fundamental requirement is the capacity for human dignity and individual accountability to directly influence and impact "partnerships of purpose" between public and private organizations. Given the full range of sustainability challenges we face at local and global scales, we cannot afford to sit idle, hoping that hot button issues will resolve, or that any one constituent will solve them. Whether we are talking about water scarcity and security, climate change and adaptation, food safety and security, diversity and inclusion, innovation and education, or healthcare and human rights, the complex and interconnected sustainability issues are growing in scale, swiftness, and severity.

This is all happening during our short lifetime, and during a period of history when global population has risen to a new peak of 7.7 billion people. As a result, human demand for natural resources to sustain our current quality of living continues to intensify. Simultaneously, global temperatures are rising, and the impacts of climate change and volatility of weather fluctuations are being felt in every region and community of the world. In an effort to adapt and mitigate these changes in our lives and to ensure human survivability, we are proactively engineering new systems and reengineering existing infrastructures and systems to ensure humans have access to portable water, adequate food and nutrition, and a less energy-intensive environment (such as in our transportation systems, homes and buildings).

Of course, this global transformation is not felt the same way in every community. Coastal regions, urban centers, and rural communities each are experiencing in real-time how to adjust to the realities of the social, economic, and environmental changes that occur more rapidly than in the past. Consequentially, humanity is facing and has to deal with gross resource inequalities, social justice, and equity challenges.

As an observer of the burgeoning "sustainability generation," I've seen a social shift from passive and reluctant thinking about tough issues like climate change to a reactionary mindset that has shaped the dialog on how to mitigate the impacts of these changes. Over the past four decades, having "sustainability" has become more mainstream, to the point where it is viewed by many as another meaningless buzzword without any true substance or teeth.

For decades I've seen many peers and professionals work hard to provide credence to the value of sustainability, particularly in the business community. For the business community, sustainability needed to show a return-on-investment (ROI), otherwise it was just another corporate objective that was a nice to have, but not a real driver of business strategy, performance, or impact. Paralleling the corporate sustainability journey were policy makers, politicians, and civil society who have also looked for more clear understanding behind the what, how, and why and of sustainability.

Whether you are at the helm of a Fortune 100 company, working in customer service for a government agency, or working as a gig-economy consultant, we are all operating in world of amazing abundance, but also high alarm regarding the limitations of natural resources and the ecologic damages that human activities have caused. It is as if we've waited for some watershed moment, a Climate Treaty, a Peace Accord, a comet striking the earth, or a zombie apocalypse to come together, assess our state of affairs without bias or blame, and finally collaborate for positive change.

Well, unless I missed it, and I'm generally glued to social media like the best of them, there has not been a singular awakening for humanity. However, there have been multiple tremors and warning signs. Whether or not the "big moment" is coming is inconsequential. Taken in totality, the social, economic, and environmental stressors that divide rather than unite humanity are evidence enough that systems are broken. That leaves us with the reality that taking action on sustainability is not a sexy Hollywood movie moment. We don't need and should not wait for some magical aspiration to tell us what to do next. Rather, we need to simply roll up our sleeves, accept that we all have flaws, and move on from where we are to empower every woman, man and child to live life with a sense of purpose and resolve for enriching their lives and the lives of others around them.

Taking action to improve your life, the quality of your community, and the state of affairs in the world boils down to a consistent assessment and conscious modification of unsustainable behaviors. As global citizens and consumers, we all have the capacity to vote with our pocketbook and our voice to effectuate economic and political change. How we treat our bodies and each other are also the most evident opportunities for improving our health and the quality of relationships in our daily lives.

Stated another way, the underlying bond between each and every human begins and ends with dignity. That is, how we treat each other and ourselves. Right now humanity is broken and afraid. We are collapsing under the weight of our own fear—a fear that is permeating from deep within an entrenched, pervasive, and insidious ignorance of greed and ego that is allowed to persist throughout the world.

Make no mistake. The forces of good and evil are at play each day throughout the world. Every day we are faced with choices and behaviors that challenge the good and evil in all of us. Fundamentally, I believe human dignity and the spirit of what is good will prevail. A "sustainability generation" has promulgated across the world to shape our future for the better, grounded by the fact that there is dignity in all living matter and that humans are the stewards of our destiny. It is up to each of us, acting in concert, as individual citizens and consumers, to ensure that humanity never falls victim to its own undoing.

Another observation is that the term "sustainability" has infiltrated the vernacular of the public. We may not all use the word the same way to mean the same things. However, the impact of human behavior on our social, economic, and environmental systems is more widely understood. As a result, there is growing acceptance that we must evolve our behaviors and practices to be in step with planetary boundaries and dynamic conditions. To that end, society is beginning to move beyond a reactionary mindset to one that is more tolerant of change and preemptive in its ability to influence global sustainability. The clearest evidence is in the proactive spirited, vocal, politically savvy youth of the next generation who are technically proficient and empathic toward local and global sustainability concerns.

For better or for worse, these young people across the globe have grown up in a digitally hyper-connected and social media driven world. From a very early age, they have become highly sensitized to the terrors and ills of humanity. They inherently see the need for change and understand they need to act. Global youth are the living embodiment of the "sustainability generation" that is using its power to influence the creation of new products, policies, and practices that do a better job of integrating sustainable thinking and innovation from the onset, and not just as a corrective action. [64]

In Summary

In the future, I would like to be more of an advocate for animal conservation. Every single part of the Earth reacts with every other part. It's one thing. Every little animal is important in that ecosystem. [Seeing the planet from above] makes you realize that, and makes you want to be a little more proactive in keeping it that way.

If I could get every Earthling to do one circle of the Earth, I think things would run a little differently.[65]

National Geographic Magazine, March 2018
—KAREN NYBERG
American mechanical engineer and NASA astronaut

After twenty years of being an observer, researcher, and a thought leader and practitioner of sustainability, I continue to believe that the fate of humans and the fate of the earth are one and the same. I have now proudly written three books on sustainability that have illuminated our current human condition and the traits, values, and behaviors we should work toward to alleviate our destruction of the environment and enable people and our planet to attain a brighter future together. I have emphasized the importance of characteristics of accountability, trust, and dignity in our relations to others, including our Earth.

But as our complex, ever-evolving ecosystem of Earth changes, too often human relations become irrational, yielding unintended and undesired impacts on each other and other life forms.

Just as the planet shields us, comforts us, and sustains our life with nourishment and resources, we must elevate our intellect and compassion to rise up and serve as stewards and protectors of the planet. As I have stated, dignity is the glue that binds humanity together. If we lose our dignity and respect for each other and ourselves and our Earth, humanity will not survive.

In the past few years a frustration and discontent has risen, touching people of all regions, cultures, ages, values, and beliefs. While the world is busting at the seams with humans, too many people are feeling fear, isolation, and loneliness, and some are experiencing severe deprivations. Rising global population and its impacts tied to our irrational consumption of natural resources has pitted us against each other and created walls that divide us and threaten our ability to have respectful discourse and compromise. We need to tear down these walls to reach across to the other side and lift each other up to a more dignified existence.

Humanity on our planet has a lot in its favor. Our collective diversity, wisdom, intellect, creativity, and sheer size can all be advantages to attain a more peaceful and sustainable world. While population growth is one of the impediments to a sustainable future because more people on Earth place greater constraints on natural resources and the carrying capacity of ecosystems, we as humans with our talents and gifts are also an incredible resource to bring positive reinforcement to the earth, its ecosystems, and our future. If we understand that humanity is a human resource inexorably linked to Earth's ecosystems and the destiny of our collective futures, we know we must commit ourselves to ending self-defeating roles we currently play out and replace them with the self-respecting role of dignity.

The world is only as irrational as we make it. The basic formula for a more peaceful, just, humane, and sustainable world is quite simple. It boils down to each of us, as individual citizens and consumers, doing our part to be kind, generous, compassionate, and caring about each other and our environment.

There is no other option for us. The earth's resources, pleasures, systems, and wonders feed our souls, nourish our bodies, and enable our procreation and sustainment as a species. Humans are not superior to other life forms. All living things are intrinsically interconnected and equal.

As a conscious species aware of the impact our actions have on each other and the planet, we need to bring a doctrine of dignity forward in all that we are and do. We have to shift the pervasive culture of negative behavior and malicious intent that has swept the world into discord.

Humanity needs more people who are unafraid of speaking truth to power and reversing our course. As diplomats for humanity, we must admit to ourselves our wrong doings and misgivings without blame for anyone so that we can collectively heal ourselves and our Earth. A long trail of emotional, psychological, and social ills have weighed down our individual aspirations, freedoms, and a collective will to serve each other and the world with grace. Now is the time for us to set our differences aside. Now is the time for us to seize our freedom and determine our fate as one community, guided by a common purpose—to restore our dignity.

Endnotes

1. Quote source, Franklin D. Roosevelt Presidential Library and Museum. "Democratic Convention Acceptance Speech." https://www.fdrlibrary.org/dnc-curriculum-hub

2. Business Roundtable, https://www.businessroundtable.org/about-us

3. Business Roundtable, https://www.businessroundtable.org/about-us

4. Business Roundtable, https://www.businessroundtable.org/business-roundtable-redefines -the-purpose-of-a-corporation-to-promote-an-economy-that-serves-all-americans

5. NASA. John F. Kennedy Moon Speech, Rice Stadium. September 12, 1962. https://er.jsc.nasa.gov/seh/ricetalk.htm

6. Smartphone Monitoring in Liberian Rainforests. Leonardo DiCaprio Foundation. https://www.leonardodicaprio.org/smartphone-monitoring-in-liberian-rainforests/

7. "Auguries of Innocence" by William Blake, https://www.poetryfoundation.org/poems/43650/ auguries-of-innocence

8. "Auguries of Innocence" by William Blake, https://en.wikipedia.org/wiki/Auguries_of _Innocence

9. Wikipedia. "If a tree falls in a forest." July 2, 2019. https://en.wikipedia.org/wiki/If_a_tree _falls_in_a_forest

10. NASA. John F. Kennedy Moon Speech, Rice Stadium. September 12, 1962. https://er.jsc. nasa.gov/seh/ricetalk.htm

11. Quote by David Suzuki. Referenced by Bruce Parry in "Why Land Rights for Indigenous Peoples Could be the Answer to Climate Change." November 29, 2016. *The Guardian*. https://www.theguardian.com/commentisfree/2016/nov/29/land-rights-indigenous-peoples -climate-change-deforestation-amazon

12. NASA, Global Temperatures. https://climate.nasa.gov/vital-signs/global-temperature/

13. Statistica. "Number of smartphones sold to end users worldwide from 2007 to 2017 (in million units)." https://www.statista.com/statistics/263437/global-smartphone-sales-to-end-users-since -2007/

14. ChildStats.gov. "Adolescent Depression." https://www.childstats.gov/americaschildren/ health4.asp

15. Centers for Disease Control and Prevention. "Drug Overdose Deaths in the United States, 1999–2016." https://www.cdc.gov/nchs/products/databriefs/db294.htm

16. Ratner, Paul. "Albert Einstein's Surprising Thoughts on the Meaning of Life." http:// bigthink.com/paul-ratner/albert-einsteins-surprising-thoughts-on-the-meaning-of-life

17. For additional information on Mrs. Eleanor Roosevelt and the Universal Declaration of Human Rights see, https://www.fourfreedoms.nl/en/roosevelt-four-freedoms/eleanor -roosevelt-and-the-universal-declaration-of.htm

18. For more information on the United Nations Universal Declaration of Human Rights see, http://www.un.org/en/universal-declaration-human-rights/

19. United Nations, Universal Declaration of Human Rights. Youth for Human Rights. https://www.youthforhumanrights.org/what-are-human-rights/universal-declaration-of -human-rights/introduction.html

20. Hegarty, Aaron. "Timeline: Immigrant Children Separated from Families at the Border." *USA Today*. June 27, 2018. https://www.usatoday.com/story/news/2018/06/27/immigrant-children-family-separation -border-timeline/734014002/

21. Hegarty, Aaron. "Timeline: Immigrant Children Separated from Families at the Border." *USA Today.*June 27, 2018. https://www.usatoday.com/story/news/2018/06/27/immigrant-children-family-separation-border-timeline/734014002/

22. Campbell, Denis. "Facebook and Twitter 'Harm Young People's Mental Health.'" May 19, 2017. *The Guardian.* https://www.theguardian.com/society/2017/may/19/popular-social-media-sites-harm-young-peoples-mental-health

23. Wagner, Kurt. 'Twitter Is Wondering Whether Twitter is Bad for Society – and Jack Dorsey Is Starting New Research to Find Out.' March 1, 2018. Recode. https://www.recode.net/2018/3/1/17067070/twitter-tweets-abuse-harassment-health-measurement-safety-jack-dorsey

24. O'Sullivan, Donie. "Facebook Just Had Its Worst Hack Ever—and It Could Get Worse." CNN Business. October 4, 2018. https://www.cnn.com/2018/10/04/tech/facebook-hack-explainer/index.html

25. Withers, Rachel. October 8, 2018. Opinion. "Facebook's Security Is So Bad It's Surprising Zuckerberg Hasn't Deleted His Account." *The Guardian.* https://www.theguardian.com/commentisfree/2018/oct/08/facebook-security-bad-zuckerberg-account

26. Baram, Marcus. "The FTC is Investigating DNA Firms like 23andMe and Ancestry Over Privacy." June 5, 2018. Fast Company. https://www.fastcompany.com/40580364/the-ftc-is-investigating-dna-firms-like-23andme-and-ancestry-over-privacy

27. Baram, Marcus. "The FTC Is Investigating DNA Firms like 23andMe and Ancestry Over Privacy." June 5, 2018. Fast Company. https://www.fastcompany.com/40580364/the-ftc-is-investigating-dna-firms-like-23andme-and-ancestry-over-privacy

28. Source: For more information on the United Nations' Universal Declaration of Human Rights, see, http://www.un.org/en/universal-declaration-human-rights/

29. Hu-manity.co, Inherent Data, https://hu-manity.co/#inherent-data

30. Hu-manity.co, #My31 App, https://hu-manity.co/my31app/

31. Syracuse University News. April 18, 2018. https://news.syr.edu/2018/04/message-from-chancellor-syverud-2/

32. Source: Muller, Jordan. Daily Orange. April 21, 2018. "SU Permanently Expels Theta Tau chapter." http://dailyorange.com/2018/04/theta-tau-chapter-permanently-expelled-su/

33. Barbiroglio, Emanuela. Forbes. December 9, 2019. "Generation Z Fears Climate Change More Than Anything Else." https://www.forbes.com/sites/emanuelabarbiroglio/2019/12/09/generation-z-fears-climate-change-more-than-anything-else/#42de76c6501b

34. ypulse. January 14, 2020. "Gen Z and Millennials Are in Agreement: They're Worried About the Future and Believe This Is the Biggest Problem They Face Right Now . . . " ypulse. com. https://www.ypulse.com/article/2019/06/25/both-gen-z-millennials-believe-this-is-the-biggest-problem-their-generation/

35. For additional information and insight, see "The Deloitte Global Millennial Survey 2019: Societal discord and technological transformation create a "generation disrupted." Deloitte. https://www2.deloitte.com/content/dam/Deloitte/global/Documents/About-Deloitte/deloitte-2019-millennial-survey.pdf

36. PR Newswire. May 20, 2014. "Warren Buffett's Secret Millionaires Club "Grow Your Own Business Challenge" Announces Grand Prize Winners!!!" https://www.prnewswire.com/news-releases/warren-buffetts-secret-millionaires-club-grow-your-own-business-challenge-announces-grand-prize-winners-259949871.html

37. By Kids For Kids, http://bkfkeducation.com/about-bkfk-education/our-story/

38. Based out of McLean, VA, Food Allergy Research & Education (FARE) is the world's largest nonprofit organization dedicated to food allergy awareness, education, research, and advocacy; the group provides information, programs, and resources about food allergies and anaphylaxis. FARE was founded in 1991 to serve as a clearinghouse for food allergy information by a parent whose own daughter was diagnosed with milk and egg allergy. For more information about FARE, see https://www.foodallergy.org//

39. Originally published as an excerpt by Impakter on May 1, 2019. https://impakter.com/dignity-medium-of-self-expression/

40. Walker, Janelle. Elgin Courier-News. February 20, 2018. Reported in the *Chicago Tribune*. http://www.chicagotribune.com/suburbs/elgin-courier-news/news/ct-ecn-homeless-new -shelter-st-0221-20180220-story.html

41. Perry, Susan. August 9, 2018. MinnPost. "Too Much Screen Time Puts Children's Health at Risk, American Heart Association Warns." https://www.minnpost.com/second -opinion/2018/08/too-much-screen-time-puts-childrens-health-risk-american-heart-as sociation-wa/

42. Worldhunger.org, "2018 World Hunger and Poverty Facts and Statistics." https://www. worldhunger.org/world-hunger-and-poverty-facts-and-statistics/

43. Worldhunger.org, "2018 World Hunger and Poverty Facts and Statistics." https://www. worldhunger.org/world-hunger-and-poverty-facts-and-statistics/

44. DoSomething.org, "Facts About Global Poverty." https://www.dosomething.org/us/ facts/11-facts-about-global-poverty
    For additional useful data and resources on global poverty see: Global Extreme Poverty by Max Roser and Esteban Ortiz-Ospina, https:/ourworldindata.org/extreme-poverty and The Hunger Project, http://www.thp.org/knowledge-center/know-your-world-facts -about-hunger-poverty/

45. McReynolds, Tony. March 27, 2019. American Animal Hospital Association (AAHA). "Americans Spent $72 Billion On Their Pets in 2018." https://www.aaha.org/publications/ newstat/articles/2019-03/americans-spent-72-billion-on-their-pets-in-2018/

46. United Nations Climate Change (UNCC). The Paris Agreement. https://unfccc.int/process-and -meetings/the-paris-agreement/the-paris-agreement

47. United Nations. Sustainable Development Goals (SDGs). https://sustainabledevelopment. un.org/?menu=1300

48. United Nations, Transforming our world: the 2030 Agenda for Sustainable Development. https://sustainabledevelopment.un.org/post2015/transformingourworld

49. The B Corp Declaration. http://www.bcorporation.net/what-are-b-corps/the-b-corp-declaration

50. Woodyard, Chris. May 29, 2018. *USA Today*. "Starbucks Anti-Bias Training: Why the Coffee Chain Closed 8,000 Stores." https://www.usatoday.com/story/money/business/2018/05/29/starbucks-closure-racial-bias -training-tuesday/650316002/

51. Consumer Affairs. June 4, 2018. "Starbucks' Anti-Bias Training Gets Mixed Responses from Employees." https://www.consumeraffairs.com/news/starbucks-anti-bias-train- ing-gets-mixed-responses-from-employees-060418.html

52. Onwuka, Patrice. June 2, 2018. The Hill. "Starbucks' Anti-Bias Training May Serve Up More Harm Than Good." http://thehill.com/opinion/civil-rights/390401-starbucks -anti-bias-training-may-serve-up-more-harm-than-good

53. Coleman, Mark. Adapted from the article originally published June 15, 2016. "A Dreamer Who Dares to Dance: Mr. Fernando Paiz and La Ruta Maya Foundation, Part 1 and Part 2." IntelligentHQ. https://www.intelligenthq.com/a-dreamer-who-dares-to-dance-mr-fernando-paiz-and -la-ruta-maya-foundation-part-1/ and https://www.intelligenthq.com/a-dreamer-who-dares -to-dance-mr-fernando-paiz-and-la-ruta-maya-foundation-part-2/

54. 2018 Trust Barometer Global Report. Edelman. http://cms.edelman.com/sites/default/ files/2018-02/2018_Edelman_Trust_Barometer_Global_Report_FEB.pdf

55. Georgia Lee. April 5, 2013. "The Golden Rule: Treat Others How You Want to be Treated. Famifi. https://www.famifi.com/1885/the-golden-rule-treat-others-how-you-want-to-be- treated

56. "Law of attraction (New Thought)." Wikipedia. Accessed May 31, 2018. https://en. wikipedia.org/wiki/Law_of_attraction_(New_Thought)

57. "The Norm of Reciprocity." Wikipedia. Accessed June 1, 2018. https://en.wikipedia.org/ wiki/Norm_of_reciprocity

58. Cavaliere, Victoria. November 3, 2014. "Brittany Maynard Ends Her Life Using Oregon's Assisted-Suicide Law." http://www.chicagotribune.com/news/nationworld/chi-brittany -maynard-dead-20141103-story.html

59. Stone, Zara. "Everything You Need to Know About Sophia, The World's First Robot Citizen." Forbes. November 7, 2017. https://www.forbes.com/sites/zarastone/2017/11/07/ everything-you-need-to-know-about-sophia-the-worlds-first-robot-citizen/#1cfced3a46fa

60. Elkington, John. June 25, 2018. "25 Years Ago I Coined the Phrase "Triple Bottom Line." Here's Why It's Time to Rethink It." Harvard Business Review. https://hbr.org/2018/06/ 25-years-ago-i-coined-the-phrase-triple-bottom-line-heres-why-im-giving-up-on-it

61. For more information on American media theorist, writer, columnist, lecturer and novelist Douglas Rushkoff see, http://www.rushkoff.com/about/ and https://en.wikipedia.org/ wiki/Douglas_Rushkoff

62. Rushkoff, Douglas. July 5, 2018. "Survival of the Richest: The Wealthy Are Plotting to Leave Us Behind." Medium. https://medium.com/s/futurehuman/survival-of-the-richest -9ef6cddd0cc1

63. BusinessWire. October 31, 2018. "Sustainable Investing Assets Reach $12 Trillion As Reported by the US SIF Foundation's biennial Report on US Sustainable, Responsible and Impact Investing Trends." https://www.businesswire.com/news/home/20181031005229/en/Sustainable-investing -assets-reach-12-trillion-reported

64. This section of the book was originally published as an excerpt by Impakter, March 11, 2019. https://impakter.com/dignity-transcends-human-behavior/

65. Drake, Nadia. "They Saw Earth From Space. Here's How It Changed Them." March 2018. *National Geographic Magazine.* https://www.nationalgeographic.com/magazine/2018/03/astronauts-space-earth -perspective/

Index

About the Author

Jacob Mroczek / Jon Reis Photography

MARK C. COLEMAN is an award-winning author and a recognized voice, business advisor, entrepreneur, and consultant on sustainable enterprise and the convergence of energy, technology, environmental stewardship, and innovation.

In 2017 Mark was recognized by Trust Across America-Trust Around the World (TAA-TAW) as a Top Thought Leader in Trust.

In 2014 Mark's second book, the award-winning title, *Time to Trust: Mobilizing Humanity for a Sustainable Future,* was published by Motivational Press. *Time to Trust* was awarded a Silver Medal by the Axiom Business Books Awards in the Business Ethics category and in 2015 was also an Award-Winning Finalist in the Social Change category of the 7th Annual

International Book Awards sponsored by American Book Fest. *Time to Trust* followed his 2012 seminal book release, *The Sustainability Generation: The Politics of Change and Why Personal Accountability is Essential NOW!* published by SelectBooks. Mr. Coleman's books highlight his perspective on holistic systems-level logic and theory for advancing humanity beyond the status quo toward more integrated models of sustainable development.

Mark's career has encompassed leadership positions with applied research, energy infrastructure, engineering, academic, management consulting, manufacturing, and government organizations. He has advised hundreds of organizations in the areas of sustainability, risk, innovation, operational effectiveness, change management, and business strategy and development.

Mark has been an active blogger with the Huffington Post, Impakter, and IntelligentHQ and has published numerous articles with leading organizations and journals, including the American Public Works Association (APWA), GreenBiz.com, Environmental Leader, *Triple Bottom Line Magazine, NOVA Holistic Journal*. Mr. Coleman also serves as an adjunct instructor at the Whitman School of Management at Syracuse University where he teaches classes in Sustainable Enterprise.

Mr. Coleman resides in the Finger Lakes region of New York with his wife Aileen and two sons, Owen and Neal.

Stay connected with Mark on Twitter: @TheSustainGen